From the
Escambray
to the Congo

Para una Profesora amiga de Cuba

Hasta la Victoria Siempre

Dreke

23-10-2002

From the
Escambray
to the Congo

In the whirlwind
of the Cuban Revolution

Interview with Víctor Dreke

Para una amiga de Cuba.

De Dra. Ana

22-10-02.

PATHFINDER
New York ▪ London ▪ Montreal ▪ Sydney

Edited by Mary-Alice Waters

Copyright © 2002 by Pathfinder Press
All rights reserved

ISBN 0-87348-947-0 paper; ISBN 0-87348-948-9 cloth
Library of Congress Control Number: 2001099857

Manufactured in the United States of America

First edition, 2002

COVER DESIGN: Eva Braiman
COVER PHOTO: Members of the Lucha Contra Bandidos (LCB) units of
Cuba's Revolutionary Armed Forces comb Escambray mountains of central
Cuba in early 1960s during operation to wipe out counterrevolutionary
bands. (*Granma*)

Maps of the Congo and Eastern Congo are reproduced by permission of
Piero Gleijeses, author of *Conflicting Missions: Havana, Washington, and Africa,
1959–76* (University of North Carolina Press, 2002), pp. 65 and 110.

Pathfinder
410 West Street, New York, NY 10014, U.S.A.
Fax: (212) 727-0150
www.pathfinderpress.com
E-mail: pathfinderpress@compuserve.com

PATHFINDER DISTRIBUTORS AROUND THE WORLD:

Australia (and Southeast Asia and the Pacific):
    Pathfinder, Level 1, 3/281-287 Beamish St., Campsie, NSW 2194
    Postal address: P.O. Box K879, Haymarket, NSW 1240
Canada:
    Pathfinder, 2761 Dundas St. West, Toronto, ON, M6P 1Y4
Iceland:
    Pathfinder, Skolavordustig 6B, Reykjavík
    Postal address: P. Box 0233, IS 121 Reykjavík
New Zealand:
    Pathfinder, P.O. Box 3025, Auckland
Sweden:
    Pathfinder, Domargränd 16, S-129 47 Hägersten
United Kingdom (and Europe, Africa, Middle East, and South Asia):
    Pathfinder, 47 The Cut, London, SE1 8LL
United States (and Caribbean, Latin America, and East Asia):
    Pathfinder, 410 West Street, New York, NY 10014

Contents

HAVANA

MATANZAS

GUANIGUANICO

HAVANA

PINAR DEL RÍO

MATANZAS

SAGUA
LA GRANDE

PINAR DEL RÍO

SANTA CLARA

CIENFUEGOS

LAS
VILLA

PLAYA GIRÓN

ESCAMBRAY

TRINIDAD

Isle of Pines

SANCTI SPIRITUS

C A M A G Ü E Y

CAMAGÜEY

HOLGUÍN

O R I E N T E

SAGUA-BARACOA

SIERRA MAESTRA

SANTIAGO DE CUBA

GUANTÁNAMO
U.S. NAVAL BASE

160 KILOMETERS

100 MILES

Cuba 1959

Víctor Dreke, Havana, December 2001.

Víctor Dreke

FOR HALF A CENTURY, Víctor Emilio Dreke Cruz has been a leading participant in Cuba's revolutionary movement—as a high school activist; cadre of the July 26 Movement and then the March 13 Revolutionary Directorate; Rebel Army fighter; one of the commanders of the fight against the counterrevolutionary bands in the Escambray mountains of central Cuba; internationalist combatant in the Congo, Republic of Guinea, and Guinea-Bissau; political leader and educator; and representative of the Cuban Revolution in Africa.

Born 1937 in Sagua la Grande in the old Las Villas province (today Villa Clara), Víctor Dreke's revolutionary activity began in 1952, when he took to the streets to protest the U.S.-backed coup of Fulgencio Batista. In 1954 he joined the Youth Movement of the Third Regional Workers Federation in Sagua, where he functioned as student secretary. He was also president of the Student Association in his high school and a member of the Guatemala Solidarity Committee, which protested the U.S.-organized overthrow of the government of Jacobo Arbenz in 1954.

In 1955 he actively supported a strike by 200,000 sugar workers, during which the participants and their supporters virtually took over a number of towns in Las Villas province, where the action was centered. He was involved in support activity for strikes by bank workers and teachers as well.

Joining the July 26 Movement after it was founded in June 1955, Dreke became head of an action and sabotage cell in Sagua la Grande. In May 1957 he led a student strike. That same year, he and other members of the July 26 Movement in Sagua la Grande founded the March 13 Movement. By the end of 1957 he had been forced underground by the dictatorship's repression.

At the beginning of 1958 Dreke became part of the "José Antonio Echeverría" and "March 13" units of the guerrilla front of the Revolutionary Directorate in the Escambray mountains. In October 1958 those forces came under the command of Ernesto Che Guevara. Dreke participated in numerous battles and skirmishes, and was wounded in combat at Placetas. Among the other actions he took part in were the capture of Báez, Manicaragua, and Santa Clara, where he was second in command of the Ramón Pando Ferrer Commando Unit. He finished the war as a captain in the Rebel Army.

In the months following the triumph of the revolution in 1959, Dreke assumed numerous responsibilities: prosecutor for the revolutionary tribunals and then chief of police in Sagua; company leader of the Western Tactical Force; head of Squadron 35 of the Revolutionary Rural Police; and Rebel Army platoon leader in the Escambray, pursuing one of the first counterrevolutionary bands there.

In 1960 he was chief of the Rebel Army's squadron in Cruces. That same year he headed a school in Hatillo to train militia members for the first "clean-up" operation in the Escambray. In that operation he served as squadron, company, and battalion leader in Las Villas, Cienfuegos, Camagüey, Oriente, and Havana. In April 1961 he led two companies of the 117th Battalion in the battle at Playa Girón, where the U.S.-organized mercenary invasion at the Bay of Pigs was defeated. He was wounded in combat. In 1962 he was promoted to the rank of commander.

When the Lucha Contra Bandidos (LCB) special units were created in 1962 to complete the job of crushing the U.S.-supported counterrevolutionary bands, Dreke became head of LCB operations in the Escambray, where the bandits were centered. He served as second in command of the LCB within the Central Army. He continued in those responsibilities until January 1965, by which time all but the last few groups of bandits had been wiped out or captured.

From April to November 1965 Dreke served as second in command, under Che Guevara, of the Cuban internationalist combatants in the Congo. The volunteers went to that country at the request of leaders of the national liberation movement there who were followers of Patrice Lumumba, the assassinated leader of the Congo's fight for independence. The task of the Cuban column was to help train the forces combating proimperialist troops and mercenaries in that country.

Returning to Cuba, he was chief of a military unit preparing internationalist volunteers. He then went back to Africa in 1966–68 to head Cuba's military mission in Guinea-Bissau—at that time fighting for its independence from Portugal—and in the Republic of Guinea. After Guinea-Bissau won its independence war, he again headed up Cuba's military mission there in 1986–89.

With the founding of the Communist Party of Cuba, Dreke helped organize units of the party within the Revolutionary Armed Forces. He served on the Central Committee of the party, 1965–75. In 1969 Dreke was head of the Political Directorate of the Ministry of the RevolutionaryArmed Forces.

In 1973 he was named chief of the newly formed Youth Army of Labor (EJT) in Oriente province. Composed of volunteer units of young army recruits, the EJT worked in the Cuban countryside on the most difficult and challenging agricultural development projects.

He graduated from the Máximo Gómez Military Academy of the Revolutionary Armed Forces in 1972 with a degree in politics. He pursued various military courses, and in 1981 he graduated with a degree in law from the University of Santiago de Cuba.

In 1990 Víctor Dreke, holding the rank of colonel in the Revolutionary Armed Forces, left active military service for the reserves. Since then he has been representative in Africa for

ANTEX and later UNECA, two Cuban corporations involved in trade and construction, building housing, schools, roads, and other development projects.

Currently Dreke is also vice president of the Cuba-Africa Friendship Association and a member of the Association of Combatants of the Cuban Revolution.

He has received numerous decorations in Cuba as well as Africa.

Víctor Dreke being congratulated by Commander in chief Fidel Castro after being promoted to first commander, early 1970s. Minister of the Revolutionary Armed Forces Raúl Castro is at right.

Armando Entralgo is director of the Center for the Study of Africa and the Middle East (CEAMO) in Havana. Born in Trinidad, Cuba, in 1937, he was active in the high school and university student movement against the Batista dictatorship in the 1950s and a cadre of the March 13 Revolutionary Directorate in the urban underground. In 1965 he was a founding member of the Communist Party of Cuba. Together with Argentine revolutionist Jorge Ricardo Masetti, in 1959 Entralgo helped launch Prensa Latina, the Cuban international press agency, and headed its Africa bureau in 1966. He served as Cuba's ambassador to Ghana (1963–66), where he welcomed Malcolm X during Malcolm's 1964 tour of Africa. Entralgo also served as Cuba's ambassador to Tanzania (1994–98). From 1982 to 1994 he was director of the Center for the Study of Africa and the Middle East in the Ministry of Foreign Relations.

Entralgo helped establish and served as head of the Africa and Middle East history department at the University of Havana, and holds a Ph.D. in African studies from Leipzig University. He is the author of numerous articles and books on Africa, the Middle East, and the Americas, including most recently the African history textbook used by the televised University for All, where he is also teaching the course in which large numbers of Cubans participate. He is a vice-president of the Cuba-Africa Friendship Association.

Foreword

IN THIS BRIEF FOREWORD to the interview with Commander Víctor Dreke—*From the Escambray to the Congo: In the Whirlwind of the Cuban Revolution*—I will limit myself to a few comments and observations that may serve to deepen the ongoing dialogue between the Cuban Revolution and the movement for national liberation in Africa, with particular emphasis on the ex-Belgian Congo.

Let me begin, however, with the struggles in Cuba against the dictatorship and the bandits. As Mary-Alice Waters writes in her introduction, Dreke was one of those "rebel-minded young people" around the world who identified with the followers of Commander Fidel Castro, above all because of the way they responded to concrete conditions of life, fighting for a more just world, one in which you could change those concrete conditions of life.

With his coup d'état of March 10, 1952, the dictator Batista imposed an unjust society. What was Cuba at that time? "Our country is a police station, with an impertinent sergeant at its head." The words of José Martí, referring to the colonial conditions of the nineteenth century, rang equally true in 1952.

In describing these rebels, Dreke is describing himself. They were young people willing to die for their country, although they didn't know the first thing about revolution, as he says with a certain irony. That new world he foresaw, full of hope, rapidly spread to the farthest corners of the island. In it, the fight against racism and other hateful forms of discrimination attracted the attention of Dreke and all true revolutionaries, regardless of their racial origin. Again, the influence of Martí was felt: "To be a Cuban is more than just being white, more than just being black, more than just being mulatto. The word 'Cuban' covers all."

The goal most sought after by young people, as well as those with more experience, was unity in action of all enemies of the dictatorship. That watchword of unity would find a convinced adherent in Víctor Dreke, from the days of his first underground activities in the student and union movements. Dreke rapidly understood how much division and sectarianism could cost the revolutionary struggle.

One dramatic example was seen when guerrilla activity began in the late 1950s in the Escambray mountains. When Commander Ernesto Che Guevara's column arrived in Las Villas, he succeeded, with relative speed, in forging a unified command under the leadership of the July 26 Movement, and in coordinating actions with proven revolutionary organizations such as the March 13 Revolutionary Directorate and the guerrillas of the Popular Socialist Party. He was unable to do so with the self-appointed and factional Second National Front of the Escambray, which was nothing but a poorly armed band of pseudo-guerrillas who had openly devoted themselves to pillaging the peasant population, forcing them to provide food and services without payment of any kind. If the peasants said no, they could be murdered. After the war against Batista was over, between 1959 and 1965, the counterrevolutionary bandits of the Escambray used the same methods as those employed by the Second Front.

This extended "training" in the struggle against bandits in these sometimes hostile mountains of the Escambray was a genuine school of counterinsurgency for a disciplined yet creative soldier like Dreke. How could it have been otherwise, under conditions created by the CIA, with its most capable bandits? Dreke would later put these experiences to good use, continuing his development as a representative of "the people in uniform," to use the words of Camilo Cienfuegos. We should not forget that the struggle against the bandits constitutes what, for many Cubans, was the longest and bloodiest chapter of open class confrontation between revolution and counterrevolution. With families and neighbors divided, and coinciding with the initiation of the Cuban Revolution's first program for the countryside, the struggle was inevitably a traumatic one.

From the fall of the Batista dictatorship, and the campaign against the bandits in the Escambray that followed on its heels, I now pass over to the Congo: the "Heart of Darkness," as Joseph Conrad would write in his memorable novel on the horrors of the Belgian colonizers, or as described in "King Leopold's Soliloquy," by the great U.S. humanist Mark Twain.

Dreke spent eight months in the Congo in 1965 as Che's second in command. If his record earned him that assignment, we could add that his activity at Che's side can broadly be described as his graduation exercise. He excelled as a military strategist, ready to confront the most difficult actions in a region of the world he came to know for the first time.

Che's presence made it necessary for the Cuban internationalists to operate on the field of geopolitics and the Cold War. They were called on for more than just giving support to the national liberation movement in that impossible and extremely vulnerable country, which the Congo has been from the 1960s until today.

A year earlier the followers of Patrice Lumumba had launched an uprising, with the goal of regaining strength in their stronghold in the eastern Congo. But they were apparently unable to organize themselves adequately and overcome old and fierce intertribal conflicts. They were again defeated, as foretold by the flood of information coming from the more than 150 Congolese miniparties. A barrier was erected against the Lumumbists. On the domestic front, they were atomized. At the same time, they had to confront a large number of mercenaries from every conceivable country, modern weaponry, financial resources, and above all, the determined hostility of the Western media.

Forces in the Congo that were possibly among the best from

the standpoint of military and political collaboration, but about whom we knew little, called on Cuba for help. Eventually, with the sole aim of helping the Congolese anti-imperialists and the progressive forces of Africa, the government of Cuba, at what it considered a positive conjuncture, decided to say yes to the Congolese request for training. The Cuban revolutionary leadership, basing itself on Martí and Marx, considered this its duty. Homeland is Humanity. It was necessary to help Africa against imperialist domination, which in its neocolonial form had similar objectives in Africa as it did in the rest of the Third World. The Cuban Revolution's fight was being expressed through its support for movements of liberation and the independence of all the peoples.

The main political ideas Dreke puts forward are rooted in the profound and historic unity between the struggle against Batista (protector of U.S. interests of every type in Cuba), the struggle against the Escambray bandits and the CIA, and solidarity with Africa's anticolonial and antiracist struggle for liberation, a struggle also linked to the fight in Asia and Latin America. In 1960–61 the Congolese political leader Patrice Lumumba and the Lumumbist guerrillas in the blood-stained Congo-Kinshasa spontaneously became the symbol of these struggles. Commander Víctor Dreke, both in his thought and in his actions, drew strength from the everyday heroism these struggles demanded.

Dreke's remarks with regard to the Cuban internationalists and his role in the Congo are important.

"Thirty-four years have passed," he says. "Every time someone interviews me about this, I try to find a way, first of all, to always tell the truth. Second, not to create confusion. And third, not to cause divisions. Because we think that everything that divides us at this time is bad. We have to unite."

The words Dreke uses to explain the history of those days in the Congo are strong and direct, yet respectful. He is of the opinion, given Guevara's demanding sense of duty, that Che blamed himself for things that were not his doing. Dreke emphasizes the importance of honesty and humility, including with regard to one's own merits. The truth must be told without deception, but also without risking the need for unity.

On this level, Dreke's position has always stood out. That is the reason for his great prestige among the troops and officers, as well as the party leadership. Also to be stressed is Víctor Dreke's ongoing work on numerous missions to countries of the region, where he is justly seen by the African people as a loyal brother. His record of collaboration with Africa is full of deeds, full of the most varied forms of solidarity. For these and other reasons, Víctor has been vice president of the Cuba-Africa Friendship Association for many years.

■

Víctor Dreke, like all Cubans on the island, is well aware of how the triumph of the Cuban Revolution in January 1959 coincided with the development of Africa's decolonization movement. As the revolution was unfolding in Cuba, seventeen countries in Africa obtained their independence in 1960 alone, and nine others would do so by 1965—the same year the last of the bandits were eliminated from the Escambray.

If we look at this from two geographic vantage points, then we can see how Africa's independence made possible our reciprocal knowledge. During the decade of the 1960s, while Cuba was emerging from neocolonialism, the majority of African states were forced to exchange a colonial reality for a neocolonial one. For this reason, among others, including the social systems in our respective countries, in Cuba in those years there was a greater knowledge about Africa than existed elsewhere in Latin America. In Africa, almost no one knew anything about Latin America.

While it is true that Che's expedition to the Congo failed, as he himself concludes in his book, it is no less true, as Dreke says, that a number of people in different parts of the world have sought to "investigate" the famous chapter of history Che headed. At the conclusion of their research, some have succeeded only in producing works and views that are tremendously contradictory.

But if what's involved is a considered evaluation of what was achieved politically by the fighters for national liberation from the time of Che's efforts in the Congo in 1965 to today, then we should look at Angola, Mozambique, Zimbabwe, Namibia, and above all South Africa. Twenty years ago no one would have thought South Africa's liberation and the defeat of the apartheid system was a real possibility. And we should remember that in this victory, the South African people had the support of combatants such as those who fought at Cuito Cuanavale.

The verdict of history is that victory rests with Che and his internationalists.

Armando Entralgo
January 2002

Cuban and other internationalist combatants in the Congo, 1965. Standing, left to right: Ramón Armas (Azima), Savigne Medina (Singida), José María Martínez Tamayo (Mbili), Aldo Margolles (Uta), Víctor Dreke (Moja), Esmérido Zamora (Asmari), Martín Chibás (Ishirini), Catalino Olaechea (Mafu), Carlos Coello (Tuma), Mariano García Rodríguez (Arobo), and Domingo Oliva (Kimbi). Squatting: Adrián Zanzali (Kasulo) from Haiti, Jerome from Rwanda, and Justo Rumbaut (Mauro).

Mary-Alice Waters, the author of the introduction and editor of this book, is president of Pathfinder Press and editor of the Marxist magazine *New International*. She joined the socialist movement in the United States in the early 1960s under the impact of the expanding mass struggle for Black rights and of the victories being won by Cuba's working people as they defended their socialist revolution against Washington's assaults. She has been a member of the National Committee of the Socialist Workers Party since 1967.

Waters is the editor of *Rosa Luxemburg Speaks* and *Playa Girón/Bay of Pigs: Washington's First Military Defeat in the Americas* by Fidel Castro and José Ramón Fernández. She is the author, among other titles, of *Feminism and the Marxist Movement* and "Defending Cuba, Defending Cuba's Socialist Revolution." Waters has edited and written introductions to *Episodes of the Cuban Revolutionary War (1956–58)* by Ernesto Che Guevara; *How Far We Slaves Have Come!* by Nelson Mandela and Fidel Castro; *Making History: Interviews with Four Generals of Cuba's Revolutionary Armed Forces*; *Pombo: A Man of Che's 'guerrilla'* by Harry Villegas; and numerous other books of speeches and writings by leaders of the Cuban Revolution.

Introduction

"WHEN I WAS YOUNG, my father used to tell me, 'Don't get involved in anything,'" Víctor Dreke recalls.

"My father wasn't for Batista, he was against Batista. But he didn't believe in anyone. 'Don't join anything,' he'd say. 'Things will always stay the same. One side wins now, the other side wins later, and the ones with money will always be in power. Study and get an education and don't mess with strikes or any of that. It won't get you anywhere. Besides, that stuff's not for blacks.'

"That was my father's way of looking at things. And I think this was how many blacks in Cuba looked at things. Until the victory of the revolution.

"Fortunately, I didn't listen."

The whirlwind events of the early years of the Cuban Revolution, along with men and women whose actions changed the course of history, come alive in these pages through the rich detail of Dreke's account, providing evidence that *sí se puede.* Things need not "always stay the same."

Rebel-minded young people the world over will find it easy to identify with Víctor Dreke and the way he responded to conditions around him. He tells how he and thousands of men and women like him—workers, farmers, students, shopkeepers and street vendors, most still in their teens and early twenties—simply began fighting for a more just world following the March 10, 1952, military coup that installed the U.S.-backed dictatorship of Fulgencio Batista.

Batista's regime quickly became one of the most brutal tyrannies Latin America had yet seen. "We were ready to die" to bring down Batista, Dreke says, "but we didn't know the first thing about revolution."

In his account of how easy it became after the 1959 victory of the Cuban Revolution to "take down the rope" that for decades had segregated blacks from whites at dances in the town squares, yet how enormous was the battle to transform the social relations underlying this and all the other "ropes"—inherited from colonialism, capitalism, and Yankee domination—Dreke captures the historical challenge of our epoch. At the heart of this book lies the willingness, determination, and creative joy with which Cuba's working people, for over forty years, have defended their revolutionary course when confronted by the imperialist empire to the north, a power whose vital interests the world over are threatened by the outreaching dynamic and ongoing example of the new class order in Cuba.

As the Batista dictatorship crumbled on January 1, 1959, in face of a rising tide of mass popular resistance and the military advances of the small Rebel Army commanded by Fidel Castro, the U.S. government accelerated efforts to defend the property and privileges of Cuba's ruling class along with the vast landed estates and industrial monopolies held by American corporations and wealthy families. To Washington's amazement, the young revolutionary government could neither be intimidated nor bought off. Every act of Yankee aggression was met by growing millions of determined toilers of city and countryside who swelled the ranks of the revolution and pushed it forward, transforming themselves in the process.

The first free territory of the Americas was born.

Decades later, Washington can still neither forgive nor forget. It continues to turn every effort to destroy the living example of Cuba's workers and farmers. It looks for every opportunity to punish them for the audacity of having thrown off the imperialist boot and making a socialist revolution on Washington's doorstep. For the audacity of neither bowing to the empire nor accepting its rules and definitions.

On July 26, 1953, when 160 mostly young, determined opponents of the Batista dictatorship simultaneously attacked the Moncada garrison in Santiago de Cuba and the Carlos Manuel de Céspedes garrison in nearby Bayamo, they were, like Víctor Dreke, still far from being the conscious communists they became in the course of struggles to come. "We learned Marxism from books, but above all we learned it from life," Cuban President Fidel Castro said twelve years later at a mass rally in Santa Clara.

What were we on July 26, he asked? "Among the books they seized from us after the attack on the Moncada barracks were books of Martí and Lenin," Castro noted, but he and his compañeros were not Marxists or Leninists. "We still had much to learn, much to understand. We understood some of the essential principles of Marxism, the reality of class society divided into exploited and exploiters. We understood the role of the masses in history. But we had not yet deepened our consciousness and our revolutionary education enough to understand, in all its profundity and magnitude, the phenomenon of imperialism. . . . That we learned about in our own flesh."

Through Dreke's eyes and experiences we see the history-shaping class battles unfold. Following the lines of his story, we come to understand how millions like him were transformed from inexperienced if unflinchingly courageous revolutionary youth into seasoned proletarian leaders of a people who have proven themselves capable of defying the demands and multi-faceted aggressions of the Yankee rulers for nearly half a century.

And we see both the shape and the scope of the revolutionary class battles still to come across the Americas and around the globe.

■

From the Escambray to the Congo: In the Whirlwind of the Cuban Revolution opens a window on one of the chapters of the revolutionary struggle in Cuba that is neither well known nor understood outside that country. It tells a piece of the story of the more than six-year-long battle to eliminate the CIA-backed counterrevolutionary bands—"bandits," as Cubans across the island came to call them. Although the bandits operated from one end of the country to the other, their actions were concentrated in the Escambray mountains of Las Villas province in central Cuba.

During the opening years of the Cuban Revolution, nearly 4,000 bandits organized in 299 groups were armed, trained, supported, and financed by the U.S. government. They were instruments of a policy of sabotage and terror designed to drain the resources and demoralize the supporters of the revolution.

The first counterrevolutionary band appeared in 1959 in the westernmost province of Pinar del Río. The last group of bandits was eliminated in the central province of Camagüey in 1965. But more than half of those counterrevolutionary forces operated in the Escambray, where over 2,000 were killed or captured, and 295 defenders of the revolution—nearly double the number of those who fell at Playa Girón—lost their lives in the struggle against them.

Víctor Dreke was commander in the Escambray region of the special Lucha Contra Bandidos (LCB) [struggle against the bandits] battalions of workers and peasants established in mid-1962 by the Revolutionary Armed Forces. He was second in command of the LCB overall.

Located in the middle of the island, the Escambray is a large mountainous region in which communications are difficult. More decisive than geographical considerations, however, were the political factors that led Washington to choose the Escambray as the base for counterrevolutionary operations.

As Dreke describes, the revolutionary struggle against the Batista dictatorship came late to the Escambray, a region long scarred by petty tyranny, corruption, and banditry. The guerrilla column established by the student-based March 13 Revolutionary Directorate began operations in February 1958, more than a year after the revolutionary war against the Batista dictatorship was already under way in the eastern Sierra Maestra mountains. The Rebel Army column headed by Ernesto Che Guevara arrived in Las Villas in mid-October, barely ten weeks before the fall of the tyranny, and unified, under Guevara's command, the revolutionary forces in the area. In the rebel-held territories, Guevara's November 8 Military Order no. 1 initiated agrarian reform in Las Villas, but there was little time to extend it, or to broaden revolutionary political work with the peasants of the region prior to the January 1 victory.

Complicating the political challenges in the Escambray was the existence of another armed group that presented itself as part of the forces fighting the dictatorship. Initially set up by the Revolutionary Directorate, and known as the Second National Front of the Escambray, it became an assortment largely of self-serving adventurers and ambitious power-seekers who turned the peasants against them by confiscating animals and crops, robbing families of supplies, raping women, and terrorizing those who resisted. After being expelled by the Revolutionary Directorate, the Second National Front continued operations in the region.

Revolutions develop unevenly. Inequalities between city and countryside, as well as social, economic, and other historically established differentiations from one region to another—and unique combinations of all these inheritances—are a legacy of capitalist relations and imperialist exploitation. How well a leadership wields state power to begin redressing such unevenness is a decisive test. As Cuban President Fidel Castro explained in a speech in Matanzas on the thirty-fifth anniversary of the 1961 defeat of the U.S.-organized invasion at the Bay of Pigs, the enemy picked the Escambray because "the Escambray was politically weak."

The counterrevolutionary bands there "had some help from the campesinos," from the peasants and rural toilers, Castro noted—"a minority of them, but support nevertheless—10, 15, or 20 percent, nobody could say exactly. But the war had developed in a different way there than in the Sierra Maestra. There was never the intense political work that had been done in the eastern provinces, and some of the groups in those areas had even committed abuses."

At the high point prior to the victory at Playa Girón, Castro pointed out, the counterrevolution "had 1,000 armed men in the Escambray who were experts in evading our forces. I won't call them cowards. There can be people who are mistaken and even very mistaken who are personally brave but not personally moral. One must never underestimate the enemy.

"But they were the opposite of us in the Sierra Maestra. In the Sierra Maestra we were always on the offensive, organizing ambushes, organizing strikes, and those people in the Escambray were always running away from the revolutionary troops." They were "waiting for the U.S. invasion," Castro said.

In late 1960, as Dreke relates, the whole world knew a landing of U.S.-trained forces was coming sooner rather than later. The revolutionary leadership decided to carry out what became known as the first *limpia*, the first clean-up operation to eliminate the counterrevolutionary bands that were being prepared as a fifth column.

"The revolutionary army mobilized the militias, encircled the entire Escambray and stationed a squad of militiamen in each house," Castro told an April 19, 1965, rally. The militiamen "went there with primers to teach the peasants to read and write. And they went there not only with the willingness to fight, but many of them put themselves to work there to help the peasants. The revolution mobilized 50,000 men. . . . We eliminated [the centers of the counterrevolution] before the invasion at Girón."

After the crushing defeat of the mercenary invasion at the Bay of Pigs in April 1961, the Kennedy administration organized once again to build up the counterrevolutionary bands in the Escambray. The bandits were able to win support from a layer of peasants because in that region actions carried out in the name of the revolution were in fact contrary to national policies being implemented elsewhere, a reflection of a broader political challenge within the revolution. Under the guise of carrying out the agrarian reform and eliminating support to the counterrevolution by a layer of rich farmers in the region, some leaders of the new government and Rebel Army in areas of Las Villas and neighboring Matanzas province confiscated crops and illegally expropriated farms.

These actions were "completely at variance with revolutionary law," said Carlos Rafael Rodríguez, at that time head of the National Institute of Agrarian Reform, known as INRA, in a report published in the May 1963 issue of *Cuba Socialista*. Rodríguez explained that resistance to these policies by small and middle farmers in 1961 led to a "perceptible drop in the planting and marketing of farm produce that was felt throughout 1962." After Playa Girón, he noted, "the CIA and its agents tried to strengthen the counterrevolutionary bands that had already been dealt a decisive blow by the beating they took in the Escambray." In response, he said, the revolutionary government "decreed the expropriation of the land of all farmers giving direct aid to the counterrevolution and of those holding land areas of 15 to 30 caballerías [500–1,000 acres] who gave them indirect aid or in some manner promoted counterrevolutionary positions." Rodríguez continued:

> But when Fidel laid out this policy adopted by the National Leadership, he made it very clear that all those measures had to be taken with the participation and consideration of the small and middle farmers, in meetings of ANAP [National Association of Small Farmers], and without harming that section, encompassing a substantial percentage of the farmers.
>
> Nevertheless, it is well known that serious errors were committed, particularly in Matanzas province. Revolutionary law was not respected. Poor and rich were hit indiscriminately, without taking into consideration all the circumstances in each case. Instead of discussing with the

farmers themselves in order to decide what measures to take, in many places it was primarily agricultural workers who were called together. Carried only by their class feelings, they always tended towards expropriation.

Until the leading cadres responsible for the policy abuses were removed in early 1962, and the policies of the revolutionary government aimed at strengthening the worker-farmer alliance reinstituted, the disaffection among a significant layer of the peasantry gave political space to the counterrevolutionary bands.

"The enemy takes advantage of our weaknesses," Castro told an April 1962 leadership meeting, in a speech published the following month in *Cuba Socialista*. "But no enemy radio, no enemy campaign will prosper where it does not have a base to prosper, where there are not many people aggrieved, discontented, disgusted—no longer with the injustice that has been done to them, but with the injustice they've seen done to someone else, and that they think tomorrow could be done to them."

The revolutionary leadership corrected course and strengthened political work throughout the Escambray, as Dreke describes in some detail in these pages. On the military front, Castro explained at an April 19, 1965, rally, "we adopted another tactic" after the victory at Playa Girón. Instead of mobilizing tens of thousands of militia troops from across the country as was done for the first clean-up operation—which had to be done rapidly because of the impending invasion—the revolution organized the Lucha Contra Bandidos battalions. Made up of peasants and workers from the area, the LCB battalions "practically swept [the bandits] off the map. They hunted them in the caves where they hid themselves, in camouflaged areas, in holes. And they put them out of action."

With the successful conclusion of the battle to eradicate the counterrevolutionary bands in Cuba, "imperialism received a lesson no less important than it received at Playa Girón," Castro told a cheering throng a few months later in Santa Clara on July 26, 1965, celebrating the capture of the last groups of bandits.

Washington learned that counterrevolutionary guerrilla forces could not prevail against the workers and peasants of Cuba, mobilized to defend a revolutionary course that strengthened the worker-farmer alliance, and with a communist leadership that by its actions had won the confidence of the masses of toilers. It was not primarily a question of military tactics, but of revolutionary class politics in the imperialist epoch. "The imperialists probably ask themselves," Castro said,

> How is this possible with the millions of dollars that were spent, with the thousands and thousands of weapons they sent and brought into the country? How can it be possible that without mobilizing any more fighters than those from the mountainous regions of Las Villas, their counterrevolutionary bands were annihilated?
>
> Guerrilla warfare is a formidable weapon, but it's a revolutionary weapon. Guerrilla warfare is a formidable weapon when fighting against exploitation, against colonialism, against imperialism. But guerrilla warfare will never be an adequate or useful instrument for counterrevolution, for the imperialists to fight against the exploited, to fight against the people. We hope they have learned this lesson well. . . .
>
> In case they have not learned the lesson, however, we are keeping our Lucha Contra Bandidos battalions organized! . . . And the peasants in the Escambray are organized into mountain companies just like the peasants of Oriente province. They are trained and armed. So for the enemy our mountains now constitute impenetrable bastions of the revolution.

■

From the Escambray to the Congo also opens a window on another chapter of the Cuban Revolution about which little has been written until recently—the 1965 internationalist mission of

128 Cuban volunteers, headed by Argentine-born Cuban revolutionary leader Ernesto Che Guevara, to aid the national liberation struggle in the Congo.

In April 1999 Guevara's assessment of that mission, written some thirty-three years earlier, was published for the first time. In writing *Episodes of the Revolutionary War: Congo,* Che drew on the campaign diary he had maintained throughout the mission. Che "subjected his notes on the struggle to a deep critical analysis," Aleida Guevara March wrote in the 1998 foreword to her father's book. She emphasized that "Che is critical and direct in the hope that his document will make it possible to analyze the errors and ensure that they are not made again."

Release of the full text as edited by Che involved "a major obligation to history" for another reason, Aleida Guevara said, since major excerpts of other versions "corresponding to Che's first transcriptions" had already appeared in print in Mexico and France.

The column of Cuban volunteers went to the Congo in 1965 at the request of leaders of that country's national liberation movement and with the agreement of numerous African governments. Its aim was to provide military training to, and to fight alongside, the uneasy alliance of forces that were part of the movement that had supported slain Congolese independence leader Patrice Lumumba. They were struggling to prevent the consolidation of a semicolonial regime supported by the country's murderous former colonial master, Belgium, and the U.S. imperialist government. White mercenary forces from South Africa and Rhodesia had been brought in to do much of the fighting.

Víctor Dreke was the deputy commander of Che's column in the Congo. As he says in this interview, which took place in Havana a few months after publication of Guevara's book, "helping to tell this story is a responsibility I have, a historic duty." Unlike Che, who died in Bolivia less than two years after the Congo mission, Víctor Dreke is able to place the experience in a much longer historical perspective.

Guevara's preface to *Episodes of the Revolutionary War: Congo* (published in English under the inaccurate title *The African Dream: The Diaries of the Revolutionary War in the Congo*) begins with the statement, "This is the history of a failure." Any importance the story might have, Che wrote, "lies in the fact that it allows the experiences to be extracted for the use of other revolutionary movements."

Guevara was unflinching and unambiguous in his judgment, Dreke notes. And it's not that Che was wrong at the time. "Every word Che wrote, absolutely every letter, without changing so much as a comma, happened the way Che said." But "he left the door open so that later others could give their opinion, and it could be analyzed with the passage of time and events."

Che "would make a different assessment if he were doing it now, " Dreke insists. "I'm absolutely sure of that. He'd continue to say we should've won, that we were fighting to win and didn't. But there are things you'll see in the book that Che blames himself for, and when you analyze the situation you'll see they weren't Che's fault at all. . . . One hundred and twenty-eight men can't change the characteristics of an African country."

Simultaneous with the volunteer mission led by Guevara, another column of Cuban internationalists—led by Jorge Risquet and Rolando Kindelán—was hundreds of miles to the west in Congo-Brazzaville aiding popular militia units in that country and helping to train and equip combatants of the Popular Movement for the Liberation of Angola. The MPLA, as it was known, had recently opened a new front against the Portuguese colonizers, who still ruled vast stretches of southern Africa. Dreke, like Aleida Guevara in her foreword to *Episodes of the Revolutionary War: Congo*, explains that the lessons learned from these initial internationalist missions in sub-Saharan Africa laid the foundations on which successful volunteer efforts were carried out over the next twenty-five years in Guinea-Bissau, Angola, Mozambique, Ethiopia, and elsewhere.

Most decisive of all was the mission to Angola that began ten years later, in November 1975, when the white-supremacist regime in South Africa, with de facto backing from Washington, invaded that country in an attempt to block the Angolan people from realizing the fruits of their hard-won independence from Portugal, the last European power maintaining colonies on the continent. The operation ended some thirteen years later—after more than 300,000 Cuban volunteers had participated in the struggle—when the South African government was forced to withdraw its troops. That withdrawal followed a crushing defeat of the armed forces of the apartheid regime at the southern Angolan city of Cuito Cuanavale by the combined forces of the Cuban volunteers, the Angolan army, and Namibia's SWAPO (South West Africa People's Organisation). In subsequent negotiations, South Africa ceded independence to Namibia as well, and the death knell of apartheid itself was sounded in February 1990 by the unbanning of the African National Congress and release of Nelson Mandela after twenty-seven years of imprisonment.

As Mandela told a mass rally in Cuba's Matanzas province in July 1991, "The defeat of the apartheid army was an inspiration to the struggling people inside South Africa! Without the defeat of Cuito Cuanavale our organizations would not have been unbanned! The defeat of the racist army at Cuito Cuanavale has made it possible for me to be here today! . . . Cuito Cuanavale has been a turning point in the struggle to free the continent and our country from the scourge of apartheid!"

In November 1985, in a ceremony marking the twentieth anniversary of the two columns that served in the Congo and Congo-Brazzaville, Cuban Minister of the Revolutionary Armed Forces Raúl Castro told the assembled volunteers that the participation of hundreds of thousands of Cubans in internationalist missions to Angola over the preceding decade

> is highly revealing, not only about the historical significance of the mission entrusted to you twenty years ago, but also about how much the relationship of forces on a world scale has evolved in favor of the causes of national liberation and

social progress, and how much our internationalist consciousness has matured.

Two decades ago more than three hundred men made up the two columns we are honoring. The highest praise we can pay to that campaign, which was a precursor, is to be able to say that every one of you has been multiplied a thousandfold in your noble pledge to pay back with your very lives, if necessary, our debt of gratitude to humanity.

Today, responding not as suffering victims but as a fighting humanity determined to resist the rapidly accelerating ravages of imperialist domination, new winds of struggle are stirring throughout Africa. This was registered in Algiers in the summer of 2001 at the 15th World Festival of Youth and Students, where young people from across broad stretches of the continent came searching hungrily for speeches and writings by African Marxist leaders such as Thomas Sankara of Burkina Faso, proletarian internationalists such as Ernesto Che Guevara, and other leaders of the modern working-class movement from its founding by Karl Marx and Frederick Engels 150 years ago to today.

Surprisingly large crowds, young and old, are pressing into theaters in the United States and elsewhere around the world to see the film *Lumumba*, trying to learn the truth about such deliberately distorted chapters in the history of our common struggles.

It is a world in which the internationalism of the Cuban Revolution, as represented by people such as Che Guevara and Víctor Dreke, will be studied and learned from with growing interest and in which the true historic measure of the Congo mission they took part in will be taken.

"Our country, the only socialist bastion at the gates of Yankee imperialism, sends its soldiers to fight and die in a foreign land, on a distant continent, and assumes full public responsibility for its actions," wrote Che Guevara in his account of the Congo mission. "This challenge, this clear position with regard to the great contemporary issue of relentless struggle against Yankee imperialism, defines the heroic significance of our participation in the struggle of the Congo."

For more than forty years, the working people of Cuba and their leadership have remained an unbending source of clarity—and decisive action—"with regard to the great contemporary issue of relentless struggle against Yankee imperialism."

In September 1990, when Washington sought cover from the fifteen-member United Nations Security Council for the murderous bombardment and invasion of Iraq being prepared by the imperialist powers, the Cuban delegation—which held one of the ten revolving seats on the council at that time—voted against the U.S.-initiated resolution. "Cuba voted against it, the only country to do so!" said Fidel Castro in a speech to the Cuban people soon afterwards. "We had the honor and glory of being the only country to vote 'No'!"

A decade later, in November 2001, Cuban foreign minister Felipe Pérez Roque began his remarks to the opening session of the United Nations General Assembly declaring, "The war in Afghanistan must be stopped." The U.S. government must halt its "unjustifiable bombing campaign against that people," which "has targeted children, the civilian population and International Red Cross hospitals and facilities as enemies. As to its methods, no honest voice would rise in this hall to defend an endless slaughter—with the most sophisticated weaponry—of a dispossessed, starving, helpless people. . . . Those responsible for it will one day be judged by history." Pérez Roque went on, in the name of the Cuban government, to strongly condemn the terrorist attacks of September 11.

Attempting to blunt the force of Cuba's unequivocal stand, John Negroponte, chief U.S. representative to the United Nations, told the *New York Times* that he welcomed the "almost universal" condemnation of terrorism and support for Washington's murderous course expressed by the representatives of governments who had spoken from the General Assembly's marble rostrum. The Cuban declaration, however, was "outlandish" and "totally unwarranted," he said. Even Iraq's "negative statement," Negroponte proclaimed, "was not as strident and vitriolic" as Cuba's.

Cuba's decades-long internationalism and revolutionary intransigence, however, are neither "strident" nor "vitriolic," let alone "unwarranted." To the contrary, for politically conscious workers, farmers, and youth the world over, the Cuban Revolution's course—as related in these pages by Víctor Dreke—remains living proof that in the tumultuous anti-imperialist battles and revolutionary class struggles to come in the twenty-first century, there are very good reasons today to "join something" and "take sides." Things will *not* always stay the same.

■

The interview with Víctor Dreke took place in Havana, October 26, 1999, with a second session on December 2, 2001. The interview was arranged with the encouragement and support of the leadership of the Association of Combatants of the Cuban Revolution, especially Division General Néstor López Cuba, vice president of its Executive Secretariat at the time of his death on October 15, 1999.

Víctor Dreke himself, with great good humor, devoted many hours to reviewing the manuscript, explaining details, and securing maps, photos, and documents.

Ana Morales Varela and Iraida Aguirrechu helped clarify and expand the contents of the interview; their knowledge and animated interest kept us all going. Each of them also provided considerable editorial help through a close read of the manuscript and assistance in locating photos, maps, biographical information, and other materials that make the book more accurate, accessible, and enjoyable to all.

Special thanks for assistance in preparing the glossary is due to Commander Faure Chomón, member of the Central Committee of the Communist Party of Cuba, who commanded the forces of the March 13 Revolutionary Directorate in the Escambray in 1958, and to Col. Armando Martínez, a combatant of the Revolutionary Directorate's urban underground, a veteran of internationalist missions, and former deputy head of the Political Directorate of the Revolutionary Armed Forces of Cuba.

Aleida March, director of Che's Personal Archive, provided several photos, including the one of Fidel Castro, Che Guevara, and Víctor Dreke that appears on the back cover, taken on the eve of Guevara's and Dreke's departure for the 1965 internationalist mission to the Congo.

The Antonio Núñez Jiménez Foundation for Nature and Humanity authorized use of a number of the historic photos in its collection. Carmen Ibáñez of *Granma*, Manuel Martínez of *Bohemia*, and Dixie López of *Verde Olivo* searched the archives of those publications to locate many of the other photos that appear in these pages and offered other assistance.

Hermes Caballero, veteran of the November 30, 1956, uprising in Santiago de Cuba, assumed responsibility for innumerable research tasks.

Luis Madrid, a staff editor of Pathfinder Press, participated in the first interview session with Víctor Dreke and was responsible for editing the text in Spanish. He was assisted by Martín Koppel, editor of *Perspectiva Mundial*, who took part in the second session.

Editing of the English translation as well as preparation of the annotation and glossary were the work of Pathfinder editor Michael Taber, who also participated in the second session.

A large team of volunteers around the world made possible the production of the book, which is being published simultaneously in both English and Spanish. Transcription and translation of the interview were the work of Marty Anderson, Eva Chertov, Paul Coltrin, Carlos Cornejo, Hilda Cuzco, Sabás Herrera, Blanca Machado, Ruth Nebbia, Andrés Pérez, Alejandra Rincón, Aaron Ruby, Mirta Vidal, and Matilde Zimmermann.

Eric Simpson designed the photo pages, and together with Mike Shur, prepared the maps. Eva Braiman designed the cover and text.

The Pathfinder Reprint Project volunteers helped in preparing the photographs, as well as copyediting, formatting, and proofreading the text, assuring that it was print-ready and substantially free of typographical errors.

The combined labors of all made possible this contribution to our knowledge and understanding of the Cuban Revolution and its place in the modern history of working people the world over who are fighting against exploitation and racism and for national liberation and socialist revolution—the only future for humanity.

Mary-Alice Waters
December 2001

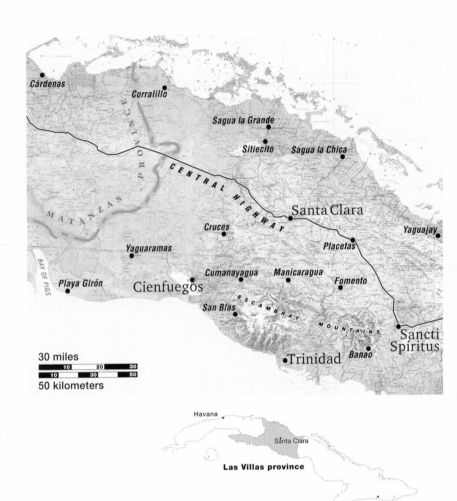

Las Villas province

'We were ready to die to bring down Batista, but we didn't know the first thing about revolution.'

On May 8, 1956, members of the Youth Movement of the Third Regional Workers Federation in Sagua la Grande mark the twenty-first anniversary of the assassination of Antonio Guiteras, a leader of the 1933 revolutionary upsurge in Cuba. The action was quickly broken up by Batista's police. In the photo are, clockwise: Víctor Dreke (holding portrait of Guiteras), Mario Sáez, Lorenzo Pentón, Roberto Sacerio, "Pintica," Miguel Mon, Humberto Rovira, and Roberto Trespalacios.

Joining the
revolutionary movement

As Víctor Dreke explains in the pages that follow, his political activity began in response to Fulgencio Batista's March 10, 1952, military coup against the elected government of President Carlos Prío Socarrás.

Batista was already well known to the Cuban people. He had headed a repressive regime from 1934 to 1944 that had been marked by brutality, corruption, and subservience to the interests of U.S. imperialism and Cuba's own landlords and capitalists. Following the 1952 coup, the Batista gang quickly moved to consolidate power and establish one of the bloodiest dictatorships in Latin America, and it did so with the full backing of Washington.

The coup aroused widespread opposition throughout Cuba. From one end of the island to the other, working people and youth wanted to fight. But the major bourgeois opposition groups and politicians opposed any revolutionary action. They steered the deepening anti-Batista energy into ineffective channels such as boycotting stores and movie theaters, refusing to pay taxes, and withdrawing money from bank accounts. They aimed to convince Washington that they, not Batista, could best defend imperialist interests in Cuba. Above all, they feared a struggle against the Batista dictatorship by the workers and peasants on the plantations, in the factories, and throughout countryside and city that could grow over into a struggle against the entire capitalist system.

Among the young people determined to organize a fight against the tyrannical regime was Fidel Castro. A member of the Orthodox Party and one of its most popular candidates in the 1952 elections aborted by the coup, Castro initially sought to convince the party

leaders to fight Batista. Having exhausted this effort, he and a hand-
ful of other young people set about creating a new revolutionary movement to do the job. By early 1953 they had organized some 1,200
workers and students, overwhelmingly young. The organization came
to be known as the Centennial Generation—named in honor of
the hundredth anniversary of the birth of José Martí, Cuba's national
hero.

On July 26, 1953, some 160 combatants, under the command of
Fidel Castro, launched an insurrectionary attack on the Moncada army
garrison in Santiago de Cuba, together with a simultaneous assault
on the Carlos Manuel de Céspedes garrison in Bayamo. This assault announced the revolutionary war against the Batista dictatorship.

The attempt to seize the garrisons and liberate the weapons inside them failed. Batista's forces massacred more than fifty of the
captured revolutionaries. Fidel Castro and twenty-seven others, including Raúl Castro and Juan Almeida, were tried and sentenced to
up to fifteen years in prison. In the face of a massive public campaign for amnesty, those imprisoned were released on May 15,
1955.

As the rebels returned to Havana, where they received a tumultuous welcome, they were already discussing the name of the organization under which the struggle would continue.

In June 1955 the freed combatants, together with young cadres from the left wing of the Orthodox Party and other revolutionary forces, formed the July 26 Revolutionary Movement. The principal leaders of the new movement were soon forced into exile,
meeting up in Mexico, where they set about organizing and training their forces to return to Cuba. Among the revolutionaries who
joined them was the young Argentine doctor Ernesto Che Guevara.

In November 1956, eighty-two of these revolutionary combatants
set sail aboard the yacht *Granma* from Tuxpan, Mexico. The expeditionaries landed in southeast Cuba on December 2, 1956, marking the beginning of the Cuban revolutionary war based in the Sierra
Maestra mountains.

■

MARY-ALICE WATERS: More than forty years after the over-throw of the Batista dictatorship, Cuba's course continues to point a way forward. That's why so many rebels and fighters around the world want to study the revolution and learn its lessons.

But revolutionary-minded young people in the United States and other countries find it hard to envision that it was people very much like themselves who joined in the fight to bring down the Batista regime, and went on to establish the first free territory in the Americas on the very doorstep of the most powerful and brutal—and the final—empire the world has known.

You were one of those individuals. How did you come to join the revolutionary movement?

VÍCTOR EMILIO DREKE CRUZ: As it happens, the very day Batista staged the coup, March 10, 1952, was my fifteenth birthday. I was born in 1937, in the town of Sagua la Grande in Las Villas province. I come from a poor, working-class family, from a neighborhood in Sagua called Pueblo Nuevo. I was born and lived in a small house with a palm-thatch roof and a dirt floor.

My father was a vendor. He sold fish from a stand in the marketplace, but he had trouble paying for the space. I found a letter written to my father in 1934, saying they'd taken the stand away from him because he'd failed to pay the fee. I still have that letter. He was told he could never again open up a stand to sell fish. I can imagine what a crisis that must have been for him.

When I was young, I remember my father used to tell me, "Don't get involved in anything." My father wasn't for Batista, he was against Batista. But he didn't believe in anyone. "Don't join anything," he'd say. "Things will always stay the same. One side wins now, the other side wins later, and the ones with money will always be in power. Study and get an education and don't mess with strikes or any of that; it won't get you anywhere. Besides, that stuff's not for blacks."

That was my father's way of looking at things. And I think

this was how many blacks in Cuba looked at things. Until the victory of the revolution. Fortunately, I didn't listen.

I'm a revolutionary because I didn't pay attention to my dad. But I'm sorry he didn't live to see he was wrong about this.

I was in school at the time of the coup. The first news we received was that Batista had seized power, and that Prío Socarrás was going to put up resistance. We heard that the students had gone off to the hill by the university steps and were asking for weapons from the Prío government to defend the 1940 constitution.[1]

Prío's government was one of those puppet regimes that existed in Latin America. In reality it answered to the United States, to Washington.

All of us at school took to the streets against Batista's coup, since it was general knowledge that Batista was bad, and we joined a political strike organized to oppose the coup. The central leader of the strike in the area was a man named Conrado Rodríguez Sánchez. He had been a peasant, a poor man, from the Santa Teresa Sugar Mill, as it was called then, in the town of Sitiecito on the outskirts of Sagua. Today it's called the Héctor Rodríguez Sugar Mill.

Conrado Rodríguez Sánchez demagogically presented himself as a proletarian leader. He wore a guayabera shirt with the sleeves rolled up and was an enemy of the suit and tie. But at his side were genuine fighters for the sugar workers and young anti-Batista rebels who thought he was a real fighter for the workers, even if not of the same stature as Jesús Menéndez or Lázaro Peña. Mr. Rodríguez showed his true colors when he

---

1. The constitution of 1940 reflected the anti-imperialist sentiment that remained deeply rooted among the Cuban people in the years following the revolutionary upsurge of 1933 that toppled the U.S.-supported dictatorship of Gerardo Machado. It provided for land reform and other democratic measures, but these provisions remained a dead letter under the successive pro-imperialist regimes. The 1940 constitution was abrogated entirely when Fulgencio Batista seized power in 1952. Its restitution was a demand of the revolutionary forces who were fighting against Batista.

ended his career together with the bourgeois and terrorist elements of Alpha 66.

The strike lasted only a few hours. Because Prío did not resist; he fled. The students were not given weapons, and Batista's coup was successful.

That same day, the army and police—which until then had been the army and police of Prío Socarrás, of Prío's Authentic Party—immediately became Batista's army and police. They backed Batista. They attacked the demonstrations we were staging and arrested a group of compañeros and put us in jail. But they released us, because the 1940 constitution said that minors—anyone under age 18—could not be put on trial.

We were a rebellious bunch, but we didn't know the first thing about revolution. We protested because we believed Batista was bad. We didn't have a clear idea of what we hoped to accomplish. I honestly think that if the Prío government had given us weapons, we would have fought against the army. We were ready to die in the fight against Batista.

So this was my initiation. From that point on we were branded as revolutionaries by the police. Every year, when March 10 rolled around, the police would come arrest us and throw us in jail.

I continued my studies and went on to high school in downtown Sagua. Then, on July 26, 1953, the Moncada and the Carlos Manuel de Céspedes garrisons were attacked.

July 26 was a Sunday. We didn't know anything about the events that day. But at dawn the following day, the police came and arrested us and took us to the police station. We didn't know why we'd been locked up. At the station we heard that "a group of outlaws" had attacked the Moncada garrison and that all the outlaws had been wiped out. That was the word used in the Batista government's official communiqué: Fidel and the group of revolutionaries were "outlaws."

Speaking for myself, I was filled with admiration to learn that a group of young people had tried to take the garrisons. Because throughout Cuba's history, a lot of people had talked about revolution. During this period in 1953—when Fidel attempted to take the Moncada garrison and, as he says, "set in motion the little engine that would start the big engine of the revolution"— there were a lot of movements that talked about armed struggle to get rid of Batista. But what they were actually doing was stealing money. They would collect money from people and buy weapons, and then they themselves would turn the weapons in to the authorities to justify not carrying out the action.

But this courageous deed by Fidel inspired optimism and led Cuban youth to admire and respect him. A path was opened up.

As for me, I was willing to give my life to defeat Batista—I had no doubt about that—but I did have doubts that anyone was really going to go up against Batista and do what they said they would do. Aureliano Sánchez Arango of the Authentic Party, for example, had talked about landing some people in Cuba to fight Batista. The same with Tony Varona, another leader of that party. But it was all a lie. It was all fake.

But Fidel Castro did come through. People now trusted him. We were confident Fidel was going to take up arms against Batista, because he'd actually done so. It was one of the events that made us more confident of taking the road of revolutionary struggle.

In 1955 the July 26 Movement was formed. That was a historic leap forward. I immediately joined a cell of the July 26 Movement in Sagua la Grande, becoming head of sabotage actions.

At the same time we continued to be part of the workers movement led by Conrado Rodríguez. This movement was affiliated to the Third Regional Workers Federation in Sagua, which encompassed the sugar workers in that area. There were nine sugar mills in the Sagua la Grande region at the time. So it was one of the most powerful sugar-producing areas in the country. The workers there were also among the most combative. The sugar workers' fight led by Jesús Menéndez had been based, in part, in this area.

Within this workers movement there were both right-wing and left-wing currents.

There was one group within the Youth Movement of the Regional Federation—which is what the youth section of this workers movement was called—that favored the electoral road. One of the principal figures they looked to was José Pardo Llada, a member of the Orthodox Party who had presidential aspirations. This group wanted to get rid of Batista, but they thought they could do so through elections.

Then there was our group within this workers youth movement, which was against the electoral road and for armed struggle. We thus belonged both to what could be called the sugar workers movement and to the July 26 Movement. In other words, we had a link between the July 26 Movement—the student struggles—and this workers movement. So I came out of this combination, this symbiosis.

The struggle was very difficult, because as soon as you planned something, the government, the dictatorship, would come after you. You had to be in hiding part of the time, fleeing, persecuted.

We organized various revolutionary activities. On May Day, for example, we would organize different actions in opposition to Batista and in favor of the working class. These were lightning events. You hardly ever got a chance to speak. The moment you assembled, the police and the army would immediately arrive, with the snitches fingering people. Events had to be planned clandestinely.

We also waged a fight to honor Antonio Guiteras, holding activities on May 8, the anniversary of his assassination. I have photos somewhere of the activities we held in 1953, 1955, 1956, where I participated in activities by the student movement in tribute to Guiteras.

Antonio Guiteras was the central leader of the revolutionary movement of 1933. For me personally, until Fidel Castro came on the scene, Guiteras was the figure I most respected and whose ideals I was a follower of. I still feel that way. I hadn't yet been born when he was assassinated in 1935, but growing up I learned the whole history of Guiteras, his activities, what he had fought for in the Hundred Days Government,[2] and I considered my-self a *Guiterista*. All these things were still a jumble in my mind. But the important thing was that I was in favor of the struggle, the armed struggle.

As a result of our revolutionary activities—the strikes, the torching of sugarcane fields, the sabotage, and all that—we were "burned," as we say in Cuba. That is, our identities became known, and we were being hunted by the police. It simply be-came impossible to function at a certain point.

In November or December 1957 a big revolutionary offensive was taking place, with sugarcane fields set on fire and other actions, in order to prevent the fake elections scheduled for the following year. Two compañeros in the cell I was the leader of were arrested.

One of the compañeros talked under torture. The other com-pañero held firm and didn't talk.

One of my friends, a young man who worked with me, came immediately to my home, which was a small room my mother and I lived in. He warned me that so-and-so had been arrested, and that afterwards the police had come searching for other com-pañeros and arrested some. We realized the man must have talked. I decided not to let myself get caught. By then, Batista's government was murdering people. I said good-bye to my mother and left the house.

I headed toward the neighborhood where I'd been born. Like the story about elephants always going back to die in the place they were born. I did so because I knew my neighborhood, I knew how I could get out. "If I can get to Pueblo Nuevo," I said to myself, "no one will ever catch me." First, because my fam-ily would protect me. And second, because I knew the area.

I took off on a bicycle for Pueblo Nuevo, for my aunt's house. I got there and told my aunt that the army was searching for me, that I had to hide, that I wasn't going to go out.

My poor aunt had been through a lot with me. Every time she

2. See glossary.

heard I was in jail, she and Cuca Acevedo, the mother of one of
our compañeros, would go get me at the police station. I had
the poor woman all tired out by then.

"You're in trouble again, what's going on?"

"Well, what can I do?" I said.

And I sat there in the house, thinking about that. Because by
then I already knew I had to join the rebels in the mountains.

Suddenly, I spotted two army jeeps coming up the street. Inside the first jeep was this compañero who'd talked. He was
sitting in the middle, between two soldiers. I'd forgotten I had
brought this guy to the house once. I'd had no connection with
Pueblo Nuevo for years.

"They're coming to get me," I said to my aunt. "Tell them I
was never here."

I went out the back, jumped over the fence, and headed for
the house of a cousin. I came in through the backyard. Everyone panicked, thinking a thief had broken in. But then they saw
it was me.

"All right, come in, sit down. What happened?" I explained,
and my cousin told me to stay in the house, not to go out.

I immediately made contact with the July 26 Movement, because my cousin, Marcelo Castillo, belonged to the July 26 Movement, although his father Florencio was a councilman for the
Liberals, one of Batista's parties. That was common during the
revolutionary struggle in Cuba: that within the same family,
some were for Batista and others against Batista. That happened
a lot in our country.

My revolutionary cousin went and told the compañeros that
the army was looking for me and that I was in hiding. That night
they moved me to the home of another cousin, where I hid out
for two days in one of the rooms, barely able to breathe.

On the morning of the second day the owner of the house
came home. He came in and started talking to his wife in a loud
voice: "I'm going to buy you furniture. I'm going to bring you
some furniture. You'll like it." And he kept talking about the
furniture. They couldn't afford furniture; they were practically

destitute. But that's the news all the neighbors heard. Because those houses are all right next to each other, they're made of wood, and everything you say in one house can be heard in the next.

The two of them went out. Later that afternoon he showed up with the furniture. A living room set, a bedroom set, an easy chair, a dresser, a cabinet, and I don't know what else. They brought the furniture into the house.

But there was a plan afoot, which I didn't know about until the furniture arrived. I hadn't been told anything. The July 26 Movement cell had devised a plan to get me out of that house and out of Sagua, because all the exits had been closed off and the army was looking for me.

What was the plan?

The first part was to arrive with the furniture and make a lot of noise, so everyone in the neighborhood would know about it. "Look, he bought furniture. He's giving her furniture," they'd say.

Later that afternoon, after my cousin had already gone back out, his wife came home. When he returned, she created a scene. Everyone in the neighborhood heard it, because that was the plan. "I don't want the furniture! Take it away! I don't want it! Besides, we can't afford it; you know we can't." She kept on and on like this, so he went and got a truck to take the furniture back.

Driving the truck was Arnaldo Arias Echenique, who owned the furniture store I worked in and who later left Cuba. He had been lined up through his brother Mario, who was a member of the July 26 Movement.

As they were preparing to take the furniture out, they put me inside the cabinet, a tiny two-door cabinet I was able to fit into because of my small size. Then they loaded the cabinet, with me in it, onto the truck, and put the living room set in front of it. That's how they got me out.

I was taken to Santa Clara, where I was picked up by a compañero named Morejón, one of the July 26 Movement's leaders in Sagua, who later betrayed the revolution.

It's a story the old people in town still talk about. "The guy escaped in a cabinet."

"I helped. I helped," everyone claims.

There are about a thousand people in Sagua who claim to have helped me escape.

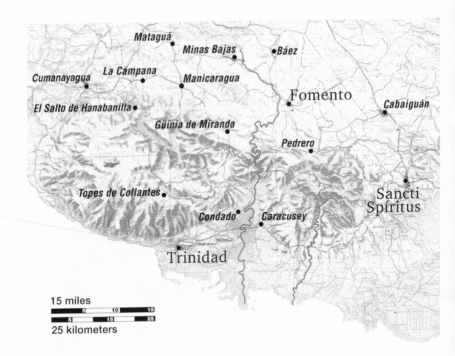

15 miles

5 10 15

5 15 25

25 kilometers

Escambray mountains

'The entire people came out in the streets and joined us.'

Víctor Dreke (right) in town square in Güinía de Miranda in Las Villas province after town was liberated by Che Guevara's column on October 27, 1958. The other combatants are, left to right, Pedro Cruz (Pelongo), Raúl López Pardo (Raulín), and José Tapia (Mandarria). Behind them is monument to José Martí, central leader of Cuba's 1895 independence war.

In Cuba's revolutionary war

Cuba's revolutionary war was in its second year when Víctor Dreke reached the Escambray mountains in early 1958, joining the rebel guerrilla forces there.

To coincide with the expected landing of the *Granma,* the July 26 Movement sought to organize armed actions in a number of cities. The most important was in Santiago de Cuba, where the movement, led by Frank País, organized an uprising on November 30.

The eighty-two expeditionaries actually landed three days later, on December 2, 1956, in eastern Cuba's Oriente province. Three days after that, Batista's troops took them by surprise. Half were killed or captured. Of those who escaped, only half were able to reassemble in the coming weeks and establish a base of operations in the nearby Sierra Maestra mountains. They became the nucleus of the Rebel Army. Among them were Fidel Castro, Raúl Castro, Juan Almeida, Ernesto Che Guevara, Camilo Cienfuegos, Ramiro Valdés, and others who would go on to become commanders in Cuba's revolutionary war.

Over the next year and a half, the Rebel Army more and more became the catalyst for the growing mass opposition to Batista. Within the towns and cities—known in the July 26 Movement as the *llano,* the plains—cadres of the movement organized effective action in support of the rebels in the *sierra,* the mountains, and prepared the conditions for an urban uprising. Other anti-Batista organizations, such as the Revolutionary Directorate and the Popular Socialist Party, were increasingly drawn into a united effort.

In mid-1958 the Rebel Army withstood and defeated a "final offensive" by the Batista army aimed at crushing the revolutionary movement. The rebels rapidly launched a counteroffensive. In addition to establishing three new fronts in Oriente province led by Raúl Castro, Juan Almeida, and Delio Gómez Ochoa, they organized two columns, one led by Che Guevara and the other by Camilo Cienfuegos, to undertake a westward invasion. Guevara's column marched to the Escambray mountains in southern Las Villas province, where he was assigned to take command not only of the July 26 Movement guerrilla column operating there under the leadership of Víctor Bordón Machado, but of all revolutionary forces. The column led by Camilo Cienfuegos had originally been given the task of crossing the entire length of the island to establish a front in the mountains of Pinar del Río in western Cuba. In October, however, Fidel Castro ordered Cienfuegos to stay in northern Las Villas province until his troops could physically regain their strength and the next stage of the campaign could be adequately prepared.

In the Escambray Guevara's Rebel Army column immediately began carrying out coordinated operations with a guerrilla front already there organized by the March 13 Revolutionary Directorate, which came out of the student movement. The Directorate had set up a guerrilla force in the Escambray in February 1958, led by Faure Chomón.

The date in the organization's name commemorated the March 13, 1957, attack on Batista's Presidential Palace in Havana organized by the Directorate. A number of its members and leaders had been killed during this attack and its aftermath, including José Antonio Echeverría, the Directorate's founding leader.

The Directorate and the July 26 Movement had been collaborating with each other since August 1956, when Echeverría and Fidel Castro signed what was called the Mexico Letter, agreeing to joint action by the two organizations to topple Batista.

As Víctor Dreke explains, by the time of the Rebel Army's westward offensive, he had joined the Directorate's guerrilla unit fighting in Las Villas.

In addition to these two organizations, in late 1958 a smaller guerrilla unit in northern Las Villas organized by the Popular Socialist Party and headed by Félix Torres put itself under the command of Camilo Cienfuegos.

Also in the Escambray was a different kind of group, one that had been expelled from the Revolutionary Directorate. It was called the Second National Front of the Escambray. This organization refused to collaborate with Guevara's Rebel Army column or with the Revolutionary Directorate. Their refusal to wage more than a semblance of a fight against Batista's troops earned them the contemptuous label of "the cow eaters," since the only casualties they inflicted were to the peasants' cattle that they rustled, slaughtered, and ate. They constantly took food and supplies from the peasants without paying.

Throughout the fall of 1958 the rebel forces in Las Villas put an ever-tightening stranglehold on Batista's army. By late December, most towns and cities in the province had been captured, and the Rebel Army was closing in on Santa Clara, the main city in Las Villas and the third most important in Cuba.

The battle of Santa Clara began on December 28. By New Year's Eve, Batista's forces in the city were on the verge of surrender. The loss of Santa Clara would cut the island in two. This development—combined with strong Rebel Army advances in Oriente closing in on Santiago de Cuba—forced Batista to flee the country in the early morning of January 1, 1959.

The forces led by Camilo Cienfuegos and Che Guevara occupied the main military garrisons in Havana January 2. As a popular insurrection and general strike called by the rebel forces swept the island, the main columns of the victorious troops commanded by Fidel Castro rolled toward Havana. The Freedom Caravan, as it was called, arrived January 8.

With the Rebel Army victorious, a new stage in the revolution began.

■

LUIS MADRID: What happened after you escaped from Sagua la Grande? How did you join the Rebel Army?

DREKE: I came to Havana looking for a contact so I could go to the Escambray, to join the rebels.

I had tried previously to become a rebel fighter in the Quemado de Güines area, about twenty kilometers or so outside

Sagua, where there was a guerrilla unit of the July 26 Movement led by compañero Víctor Bordón. But part of the group I belonged to, which was also in the July 26 Movement, did not support armed struggle. They would keep telling compañeros who wanted to take up arms: "Not today, maybe tomorrow— or the day after tomorrow."

I made contact here in Havana, and I left for the Escambray mountains.

WATERS: Did you go with members of the July 26 Movement or the Revolutionary Directorate?

DREKE: Let me explain.

The July 26 Movement got me to Havana, and then they took me back to southern Las Villas, to Cienfuegos. There I met with several leaders of the July 26 Movement at a medical clinic along the main street. One of these leaders was Víctor Paneque, who was in charge of sabotage actions for the movement in Las Villas province at the time, but who later betrayed the revolution. I met with him there, and he sent me to the Escambray. That same day three of us—including Armando Choy, who is now a brigadier general in the Revolutionary Armed Forces—started out for the mountains.

So I arrived in the Escambray as a member of the July 26 Movement.

What was happening in the Escambray at that time? All the fronts were united; there was one single front. The March 13 Revolutionary Directorate had opened the front in February 1958, but you could see compañeros wearing the July 26 armband and others wearing the March 13 Revolutionary Directorate armband. When I arrived, all the compañeros were there together. I was given a revolver, and several days later they took me out on my first action.

As we headed out, the combatants were divided up, with a captain commanding each group. My first action was the attack on the electrical plant in the town of San Blas, an attack led by Víctor Bordón.

The next time they sent me with Tony Santiago, who belonged

to the March 13 Revolutionary Directorate. I liked the way Tony Santiago conducted himself. I was impressed by his discipline, his personal courage. Planes were flying overhead, and I remember he said to us: "We have to shoot at the planes, don't be afraid of them." I came to really admire this man who was not afraid. In addition, I too had come out of the student movement. So I stayed there with that unit. That's why I say I was a combatant of the March 13 Revolutionary Directorate.

MADRID: What actions did you participate in?

DREKE: I took part in various engagements, and was wounded in combat at Placetas. I was hit twice.

That action took place on October 13, 1958, as Che's and Camilo's troops were advancing in their invasion westward from the Sierra Maestra.[1]

From as far away as Camagüey, all the dictatorship's forces in the center of the country were set against those compañeros, who were fighting to reach Las Villas and Pinar del Río provinces; the latter was Camilo's plan. To assist their advance, the leadership of the March 13 Revolutionary Directorate decided to carry out several actions to attract the army's attention and relieve the pressure on the troops of Che and Camilo.

Two targets were chosen: Fomento and Placetas. Our idea, of course, was not to capture and hold these towns. We attacked Placetas, and Faure Chomón led the attack on Fomento, where they took the police station.

Placetas is on the Central Highway, some thirty kilometers east of Santa Clara. It was a two- or three-day march to get there. The action on October 13 took place during a downpour.

Compañero Ricardo Varona, who led the attack, was from Placetas, but the rest of us weren't, and we didn't know the streets. We began to advance, but suddenly, before reaching the

---

1. For an account of the invasion by the Rebel Army columns of Che Guevara and Camilo Cienfuegos, as well as of the entire Las Villas campaign and the battle of Santa Clara, see Ernesto Che Guevara, *Episodes of the Cuban Revolutionary War 1956–58* (Pathfinder, 1996).

police station, we came upon a car we could barely see through the pouring rain.

The car approached, shining its headlights on us. We were practically blinded. We jumped down from the curb and ordered the driver to halt, without knowing who was in the car. The occupants responded, asking who we were, and we kept asking them who they were. Then one of them shouted, "Police!" We responded "Directorate!" and a shootout began.

We moved in on the patrol car, and as we advanced, firing on those inside, José "Pepe" Tapia, one of our fighters, tried to fire his Thompson machine gun at point-blank range. But the gun jammed. It wouldn't fire because it hadn't been properly cleaned. I was standing next to Pepe, and the enemy opened fire. I was shot in the leg and took another bullet in my side, just missing my lungs.

I nearly lost my life, but we got the police who were in the car, and we captured it. The compañeros got me out of there, wounded. We also took a policeman who was bleeding. What we didn't know was that inside the car was the chief of police, who was also wounded. We found that out only later. He was one of the dictatorship's notorious murderers.

They got me out of there, gave me first aid, and brought me to the Escambray mountains, where I was attended to.

We've looked for this military action in the news articles and the histories on that time, and it's virtually ignored. It's not that Batista didn't pay any attention to it, but he didn't want it to be known. Because it was a big thing to admit that the rebels had been right there in Placetas and in Fomento. This was especially true of Placetas, a city in the middle of the island, right on the Central Highway. So the government completely suppressed news of this action.

WATERS: The arrival of Che's and Camilo's columns upped the ante. The fighting in Las Villas in the last months of 1958 was intense. Did you recover from your wounds in time to join that campaign?

DREKE: Prior to the battle of Santa Clara I was involved in

various actions, one of which we called "the Rescue." It took place on December 17, 1958.

Che was in the Escambray, Camilo was in northern Las Villas, and we were on the offensive. Many villages and towns had been liberated, many military posts had been taken, and the dictatorship's army from the central part of the island had massed in Santa Clara.

One of our compañeros was being held prisoner there in Santa Clara, and he was in danger of being murdered by Batista's thugs. His name was Joaquín Milanés, but we called him "the Magnificent."

Milanés had been taken prisoner in the wake of an action in Havana several months earlier. It was an attack on Santiago Rey, Batista's minister of the interior. Rey was attacked right in the center of the city, on 23rd Street, by Milanés and several other compañeros, including Gustavo Machín, who later died in Bolivia alongside Che. The attack failed. They weren't able to execute Rey, and Milanés fled in order to join up with the struggle in the Escambray. He ended up in Sancti Spíritus, which was near where the Directorate had its main command.

One day Milanés apparently felt cooped up and went out for a walk. He got caught in an army sweep. All of a sudden the army appeared in the street checking everybody's papers like crazy, without any idea who they were stopping. Milanés was carrying a .45 caliber revolver, and he was charged with carrying a firearm without a license and taken prisoner. He of course didn't tell them he was Joaquín Milanés, and they didn't know he had anything to do with the attack on Rey.

After a couple of months, however, his captors found out who he was, that he was a fugitive they had been searching for and wanted to kill. So they arranged for Masferrer to have his goons take Milanés out and murder him.[2] Faced with this situation, we made a decision to organize a commando raid to rescue

2. Rolando Masferrer was a wealthy pro-Batista politician who led a right-wing paramilitary force of some two thousand men known as "Masferrer's Ti-

him. I was picked as one of four compañeros to carry out this action.

On December 16 we had taken the village of Báez. While there we heard that the next day, the 17th, they were going to put Milanés on trial, and by then we'd organized the rescue operation. A guerrilla captain nicknamed "Mongo"—Ramón González Coro—was designated head of the operation. Then there was Raúl López Pardo, nicknamed "Raulín," who was a lieutenant in our unit; Roberto Fleites, a compañero who was later killed in the battle of Santa Clara; Osvaldo Ramírez, who later betrayed the revolution and became a notorious assassin in the Escambray; and me.

Actually, Roberto Fleites was not supposed to be part of our operation. He had just carried out another action, bringing to justice an airplane pilot who had killed a lot of peasants in the Escambray. After Fleites killed this pilot, he ended up in the Escambray. He needed to return to Santa Clara to carry out another action, however, so he grabbed a ride and offered to help out with the rescue mission. But we told him no, that he had another, more important mission. Besides, he was from Santa Clara and everyone there knew him, which would have been a problem.

We were to get the help of Mercedes Garrido, a revolutionary and a lawyer in Santa Clara. She would serve as our contact.

On the morning of December 17 we reached Santa Clara. The idea was to carry out the rescue when we got to the courthouse. We were supposed to get there at 8:00 a.m., which was when they were scheduled to take Joaquín from the jail to the courthouse, located on the same street. The time before, only two police had escorted Joaquín, and the trial had been postponed. But this time

gers," which worked closely with the dictatorship's army. During Cuba's revolutionary war, the *masferrerista* gangs functioned as death squads, torturing and murdering hundreds, if not thousands, of the regime's opponents. Their principal source of income was from gambling, prostitution, and extortion.

they knew the identity of the prisoner, that he was Joaquín Milanés. So there weren't just two police. There were more, and besides that, instead of moving him at 8:00 a.m., they took him to the courthouse a lot earlier—six or seven o'clock.

The streets that led into Santa Clara past the courthouse had been closed off because the offensive was already under way. A number of villages and towns in Las Villas province were already in our hands, and the army had concentrated its forces in Santa Clara. So additional government security measures were in effect that we didn't know about. In our eagerness to rescue our compañero before he was murdered, we hadn't adjusted our plan to the new situation.

When we got to Santa Clara, to the street we had to go down, it had been blocked off. But at the barrier was Sebastián Nieves, who had been sent to contact us.

"The street's closed off, go over there," Nieves gestured. "The prisoner isn't in the jail anymore, he's already at the courthouse."

All our plans had to be changed. Our idea had been that when Joaquín came out of the jail with the police, we would drive down the street in the opposite direction, aiming our guns on the police from inside our car and grabbing Joaquín. If the police put up any resistance, we would have to kill them; we knew that. It was supposed to be a quick, lightning strike, without giving them time to resist.

But that wasn't to be; everything had changed. It wasn't going to happen at the jail or in the street. It was going to happen at the courthouse. Mongo decided—and we all agreed—that in spite of the new situation, we would stay and rescue Joaquín.

One reason is that some months earlier several compañeros had tried to carry out a similar action. When they got to the spot there was a lot of confusion . . . yes they could rescue him, no they couldn't . . . and in the end they didn't do it. Personal courage was a standard we all aspired to; the squad had been chosen on that basis. All of us would have been ashamed to return without the compañero we had come to rescue. It was a matter of principle, for all of us.

So we decided to wait until the court proceedings were over. We parked the car next to the courthouse. We had already left the other compañero, Roberto Fleites, at the entrance to the city, even though he wanted to come with us. We dropped him off on the way into town and parked alongside the courthouse, right near a school.

Then the long wait began—from a little after 8:00 a.m. until well after 12:00. You can imagine the tension we felt, in the middle of a city full of soldiers, sitting there, with a machine gun on our laps. Mongo and Raulín, carrying revolvers, went into the courthouse, where they killed time and hung around talking to people.

The Santa Clara courthouse had several floors. The army had positioned a .30 caliber machine gun on the roof, and there were several soldiers up there. Down the street was a cafeteria.

It must have been about 10:00 or 11:00 a.m. when two jeeps arrived plus a car, with people wearing civilian clothes and big hats, some of them in guayaberas. They were Masferrer's Tigers, the ones who were going to take Milanés away and murder him after the hearing. They went for coffee, and then began to walk around the area. With us still sitting in the car! But they didn't mess with us and we didn't mess with them. It's possible one of them noticed us and thought we were thugs too, because of the machine gun we had.

Sometime after noon, maybe about a quarter to 1:00, the action took place. Knowing the dangerous situation we faced, we were all very tense.

We were worried above all that the children at the school right there would be coming out just when the time came for us to strike. There was sure to be fighting, and those kids would be caught in the crossfire between the army and us. That was the main thing we were really worried about. Luckily, the action took place before school let out.

Finally the Magnificent came out of the courthouse. They had released him along with a group of compañeros from the July 26 Movement, who had also had their hearing the same day. That was their plan. They'd let him off and he'd "disappear." Mas-ferrer's goons would kill him and he would never be seen again. No one would know what happened to him.

Joaquín knew something was up as soon as he left the court-house and saw Mongo and Raulín standing there. He knew they'd been in the mountains. But there they were with their beards shaved off, so he knew they'd come looking for him. There was no doubt in his mind.

Mongo and Raulín went into action. They jumped the police and succeeded in wiping out two of the soldiers. Joaquín him-self was able to grab one of the soldier's revolvers. I did the task assigned to me, which was to cover the getaway. I got out of the car and began firing my Thompson, the same one that had jammed in the fighting in Placetas. I began firing at the court-house building, and at the soldiers who were outside the court-house and in the cafeteria.

The compañeros made it to the car and began to get in. When they were almost inside, someone came running toward us car-rying a revolver. We were about to shoot, but it was our com-pañero Roberto Fleites whom we'd dropped off at the entrance to the city. He hadn't left the area, and when he saw we were in a shootout with the army, he took out his revolver and joined in.

Roberto got in the car. Mongo, who was just about inside too, made a gesture, and we realized he'd been hit. I remember Mongo saying to Joaquín, "So, buddy, here you are with us." Mongo began sweating profusely.

We started off down the Santa Clara highway in the direction of Manicaragua. It was around ten minutes to 1:00.

We reached Pico Alto, where we attended to Monguito, who was almost dead. He was covered in sweat. We looked for Humberto Castelló, our doctor, but he wasn't there. He was in Báez, the town we'd taken the day before. This was something else we hadn't foreseen: the need to have our doctor close by.

So we decided to go look for a doctor in Mataguá. As far as I know he was the only doctor in town. We knocked on his door.

"You have to come with us." He was willing to come, but we took him "prisoner" to avoid problems for him. By the time we got there Mongo was dead. We took his body to the town of Báez.

Mongo was one of the most heroic of our compañeros, a great leader. He was twenty-seven years old and in his sixth year of medical school. He was one of the best compañeros of our group. Monguito died right there among us, without our being able to do anything.

Afterwards there were several more actions, among them the capture of Manicaragua, on December 23, when we were already preparing the attack on Santa Clara.

WATERS: Were these actions carried out by troops from the Revolutionary Directorate? Or were they joint actions with the forces of the July 26 Movement? What were the relations between the two?

DREKE: After Che arrived in Las Villas in October, all the forces of the July 26 Movement and March 13 Revolutionary Directorate came under his command. At the same time, each of the columns continued to decide the tactics necessary to successfully carry out the actions assigned to it.

On November 22, 1958, we had carried out the first joint action of the Directorate and the July 26 Movement, an attack on the Caracusey garrison. One group was under the command of Angelito Frías of the July 26 Movement and the other was under the Directorate's Rolando Cubela, who later betrayed the revolution.

On December 23, as I said, we were in Manicaragua, getting ready for the attack on Santa Clara. After we had been there a little while, precisely as we were preparing the battle, the Second National Front of the Escambray showed up to commit crimes and abuses, as they were accustomed to doing. Their group consisted of Jesús Carreras and several others, including William Morgan, who was an American. We'll talk more about these people shortly, when we get to the bandits.

The Second Front wanted to blow up the wooden bridge between Seibabo and Santa Clara. We had a confrontation with them over that right there in the street, and we kicked them out of Manicaragua. There was no other way of dealing with the problem. We prevented them from blowing up the bridge.

Of course, we didn't tell them anything about our plans to attack Santa Clara. We just told them that since we were the ones who had taken Manicaragua, it was ours; those were the rules of the game. They picked up and left. We already had guards stationed on the bridge, and we gave the order that no one was to be allowed to blow it up.

Later that same night, at about 9:00 or 10:00, we heard some shots, coming from the direction of Santa Clara toward Manicaragua. The shots seemed to be coming from the bridge where we had positioned our guard, or from nearby.

We thought it was the army returning, and that we would have to take them on. We came out onto the highway, where we positioned ourselves against some walls at the entrance to the town. We were waiting there, with no trenches or anything. In the streets you have to fight face to face; you can't hide in a trench, since there aren't any.

But the shots turned out to be coming from Sinesio Walsh, one of our own men, who later became one of the first bandits in the Escambray. Sinesio was driving along drunk from Santa Clara toward Manicaragua, and he came into town firing off shots.

We stopped the car and Sinesio got out. There was a huge shouting match, and we made him leave.

Sinesio Walsh was from the July 26 Movement. But because of the united front between the Revolutionary Directorate and the July 26 Movement, the latter's troops were camped near ours. We were always looking for ways to be more integrated and better able to act in a united way.

Members of Sinesio's unit would find out about actions we were carrying out, and they'd come along with us. Sinesio wouldn't want to go, but some in his unit would say, "We're going with you guys." There was no differentiation among any of the combatants at that time. All of us were together; there was genuine unity.

We later found out that when we had gone to attack the Mataguá garrison a few days earlier, Sinesio—who was a friend of the chief of the Batista army post in Mataguá—had told the enemy we were going to attack the garrison. When we got there, the chief had fled. We learned all this two years later, through Sinesio's own statements at his trial.

The Batista soldiers were all his good buddies. He couldn't warn them in Manicaragua, since we carried out the attack there on the spur of the moment. But every time he could do so, he did.

MADRID: The Rebel Army victory in the battle of Santa Clara was one of the decisive events of the Cuban Revolution. It sealed the fate of the Batista dictatorship and demonstrated that the Rebel Army had the support of the majority of Cuba's working people.

Tell us about the battle of Santa Clara from your perspective.

DREKE: I was a member of the Ramón Pando Ferrer Commando Unit headed by Raúl Nieves, the same one that had attacked Manicaragua. I was second in command. The unit had two objectives. First was to carry out actions in the greater Santa Clara area. We planned later to divide in two, and I was to take part of the commando unit and head for Sagua. That's what I wanted: go to Sagua, the town where I was born, and fight there. The idea was to create the conditions there for a guerrilla unit to operate. We had already designated Alfredo Salgado and Mario Arias to work there until our arrival.

We went into Santa Clara a number of times prior to the main attack. We burned down a restaurant, and another time the television transmission station. Once we went into a house of prostitution and threw out all the pimps—just threw them the hell out. We sent the women home and closed the house down. We did several other things like that before the main attack began.

On December 28, around 8:00 a.m., we entered Santa Clara. We were to enter along the Manicaragua highway, with the mission of attacking the headquarters of Squadron 31, and also the headquarters of the "little horses"—which is what we called the motorcycle cops.

Our first clash was with an army patrol. Then planes began bombing us and two compañeros were wounded. It wasn't easy to get from one place to another, but we had the support of the people, who were joining with us. The headquarters of Squadron 31 faced an open square, so we had to move through houses, one after the next, to get there. We got help from a resident named Noemí, and a compañero named Celestino, who both later joined the movement.

"Come through here," Celestino said, turning over his house to us, which faced right onto the Squadron 31 headquarters. So we positioned some of the compañeros there. Nieves and I headed for a different spot with another group, and began the battle.

It's important to explain what happened next, because a wonderful compañero lost his life there. The army came out with the first set of light tanks. The people had already joined us—the *milicianos,* as we began to call them at the time, although we hadn't yet officially set up the Revolutionary National Militia. In Santa Clara the entire people came out in the streets and joined us, acting as the incipient militias of the revolution. The job we gave them was to make Molotov cocktails, since they didn't have weapons and we didn't have any to give them. We sent them off at about 10:00 a.m. to make Molotov cocktails.

They went looking for gasoline, looking for all the things they needed, and started making Molotov cocktails. But then the army came and killed a group of *miliciano* compañeros. The survivors came back to the trench where we were dug in and told us what had happened.

There was nothing else to do but send someone with them. Compañero Roberto Fleites volunteered—the same one who was with us during the rescue of the Magnificent.

"I'll go take care of it," he said, swearing the way we Cubans do. "I'll make the Molotovs. Don't worry about it, I'll go."

And he took off with his weapon, taking five or six of those compañeros with him.

After half an hour or so, one of those compañeros came running up, shouting.

"Roberto has been wounded!"

"Where is he?"

"There's nobody who can get him out of there. He's wounded real bad."

What had happened? Just as Roberto was about to return with the Molotov cocktails, one of the tanks came out, and he exchanged fire with it. Roberto fired at the tank and the gunner shot him. He fell face down still holding his M-1.

We had to get him out; we couldn't leave Roberto there. I had a choice: either I had to send someone to get him, or go myself. As head of the group—right then Nieves was on another front—I made the decision that I would go.

"Look, Nieves isn't here," I told compañero Roberto Sacerio. "If something happens to me, don't come after me. Leave me there, because otherwise everyone's gonna get killed. Go find Nieves."

So I went.

I made it all the way up to compañero Roberto's body. It was horrible. The tank blast had blown off part of his face; he was dead. I dragged the body over to an area where compañeros could help me, and we buried him there.

Today that tank is on permanent display in Cadenas Plaza in front of the University of Havana. Some students probably don't realize it's the very same tank that killed Roberto Fleites.

On the second day of the battle, Che and his troops toppled and captured the armored train Batista's army had in the city. Taking over the train gave us a big advantage. Che sent us a large supply of ammunition and other weaponry. Somewhere I still have a list of the ammunition Che sent us to distribute to the troops. Before that, we were almost out.

In addition to the weapons and ammunition we got from the train, Faure sent us some from Trinidad that day. I was rewarded

Cuba Rebels Driven From Santa Clara

4,000 Casualties Reported in City; Batista Troops Pressing Attack

The United States says it will not intervene in the Cuba struggle—Page 10.

Gen. Batista's two young sons on a New York sight-seeing trip—Page 10.

By The Associated Press

HAVANA, Dec. 31.—Government troops, backed by armor and planes, hammered retreating rebel forces around Santa Clara tonight and drove them eastward out of Las Villas Province.

The army said the rebel bid to seize Santa Clara, cut Cuba in two and threaten Havana had been crushed.

As President Fulgencio Batista's army pushed rebel leader Fidel Castro's fighters toward Camaguey and Oriente Provinces, the government called on its forces to keep on fighting until the revolutionary movement is utterly wrecked. A source close to President Batista said:

"There will be no New Year's holiday and no truces or respites for the rebels."

President Batista remained in the Presidential Palace amid reports he hoped to announce a sweeping victory over Castro's insurgents by the dawn of the new year.

A spokesman for the President said the government had smashed an attempt to seize Santa Clara, capital of Las Villas Province. Earlier reports said the rebels were fighting a rear-guard action in the battered old city.

Santa Clara's streets were described as strewn with dead and wounded. Government informants estimated that 3,000 rebels had been killed or wounded. They indicated government casualties were at least 1,000.

Once rebel forces are pushed into Camaguey, the government expected their flight toward easternmost Oriente Province would gain momentum. Camaguey is the heart of Cuba's flat cattle-raising country where rebels would have little chance against armored forces and air attacks.

Presidential Palace sources emphasized the drive would be intensified once the rebels were pushed into Oriente, to destroy their strongholds there. Insurgents still have the bulk of their forces in Oriente. They have entered or occupied a half dozen cities there and isolated the city of Santiago de Cuba. Some positions were given up by the government to rush reinforcements to Santa Clara.

President Batista sent Maj. Gen. Jose Pedraza, known as an iron-fisted fighting man, to

See CUBA—Pg. 18, Col. 4

On January 1, 1959, as the dictatorship's army crumbled and Batista fled Cuba, U.S. newspapers ran this Associated Press dispatch "reporting" the defeat of the Rebel Army in Santa Clara.

with a .30 caliber machine gun. One of my helpers was Gustavo Castellón, "the Mayaguara Horse," who we'll talk about later when we get to the struggle against the bandits.

In those days we were novices. And when you don't know much about a weapon like this, it seems really impressive. Captain Chino Figueredo was the one who brought me the machine gun. He also brought a 71 mm. cannon, but I liked the .30 caliber machine gun better because it fired more bullets. I was a twenty-one-year-old without much experience, and I had dreams of firing off lots of bullets.

"Don't keep your finger on the trigger," Chino warned me, "because if you do you'll run out of ammunition. What's more, the enemy will be able to locate your position and shoot you." He also recommended I fire only in short bursts. Otherwise the gun would become too hot.

I positioned the machine gun in the window of a house. I didn't know anything about regular warfare, so for protection I piled up three or four mattresses we'd taken from the beds inside the houses. As soon as I began firing at the garrison, of course, they immediately figured out where we were, and all the mattresses were shot to pieces.

Moments later a tank rolled up, and the soldiers came out firing at us, backed up by planes. One comrade was wounded. When they opened fire, I ducked, throwing myself to the ground. I kept firing, even though the grip on my .30 caliber machine gun became too hot to handle. We then moved to another house, where I positioned myself on the second floor in order to fire at the aircraft. That's the way it went up to the last day.

By this time, some compañeros from the July 26 Movement had joined us in our assigned battle zone. I think Alfonso Zayas was there, together with several others.

By dawn on January 1 we had both Squadron 31 and the motorcycle cops completely surrounded.

That morning we saw white flags on the Squadron 31 headquarters. We didn't know Batista had fled. We just kept fighting against Squadron 31, and had them surrounded. The army had already retreated into their barracks, and we kept shooting to keep them from coming out.

At that point we had no idea we were going to take Santa Clara in four or five days. I don't think anyone would have imagined it because of the number of army troops they had concentrated there, compared to the size of our forces.

I don't think even Che, who was commander in chief of the whole operation, had figured out we were going to be able to take Santa Clara in four or five days. I'm sure he thought it would be a struggle of many days, or perhaps even months, and that we were going to suffer huge casualties. That's what we all believed at the time—that practically none of us would come out of the battle alive.

So when we saw the white flags, we decided that Nieves and several others of us should go over there. I gave my .30 caliber machine gun to another compañero, grabbed my old Thompson, and went into the Squadron 31 headquarters with the group. Entering from another direction at the same time were compañero Juan Abrantes, "The Mexican," and the future traitor Rolando Cubela.

It was only then—inside the squadron headquarters—that we heard the news. On the radio they were saying Batista had fled. The soldiers were already disarmed; they had simply thrown down their weapons.

That's how the triumph of the revolution caught us.

WATERS: You must have met Che for the first time during these months.

DREKE: I met Che in October 1958. It was some time between October 20 and 25. I saw him for the first time in Dos Arroyos, the Directorate's camp. He and the rest of his column had reached the Escambray a few days before, and one of the first things they did was come and stay in our camp. They arrived at the "Joe Westbrook" School, which the Directorate had set up there for giving classes to the peasants, teaching them to read and write.

One of the first meetings Che had was with Faure and the leadership of the Directorate. There's a photograph of our troops, those of the Directorate, and those led by Che. We welcomed Che in the manner we felt he and his troops deserved after coming from Oriente, breaking through to help bring freedom to Las Villas and to Cuba. We opened our arms to them with the little we had. Whatever we did have—clothes, shoes—we made available to Che's troops, since they arrived in really bad shape. During the trip they had lost everything. They lacked drinking water, they'd crossed through swollen rivers. As a result of the battles, a number of men were wounded. Yet they came.

I was in the camp. I'd been wounded on October 13, a few days before. By then I was getting better, but I was still in the camp. I had been assigned head of services, head of the warehouse and everything in it. They'd given me that responsibility so I had something to do while I was convalescing.

When Che arrived at our Dos Arroyos camp, it really made an unforgettable impression on me. Because after greeting me, Che asked whether I could let him use a typewriter for a few minutes, so he could write something. He also noticed I had been wounded and checked my wound.

"It's fine," he said. "There's no problem. Soon you'll be able to fight again."

We had been told about Che, but before then I really had no idea who he was. He was unknown in Las Villas province, as well as in Cuba in general; that's the historical truth. That shouldn't be falsified. He was known by the compañeros who came with him, who fought with him in the Sierra, but the rest of us didn't know him.

There was an Argentine, a foreigner—that's all people said.

And then to see this man concerned about my wound, asking what had happened to me, how I had been wounded. Giving words of encouragement, saying I wasn't seriously hurt, that I was fine. Asking permission to borrow a typewriter "just for a moment," after we had already said everything in our camp was at their disposal.

That's how I met Che for the first time.

MADRID: How was the collaboration between the Revolutionary Directorate and Che's troops organized?

DREKE: An agreement for joint action, known as the Pedrero Pact, was signed by the March 13 Revolutionary Directorate and the July 26 Movement on December 1. This followed a meeting presided over by Che and by Faure Chomón. A few days later the Popular Socialist Party also signed on.

After that agreement was concluded, the troops were divided up, all under the unified command. So-and-so goes with this group for that zone, and so-and-so goes with that group over there.

The ones who Che's troops couldn't unite with were the Second National Front of the Escambray, the ones known as the "cow eaters." These people had already threatened to take Che prisoner and wipe out his column.[3] But the rest of the Escambray was divided up, under a single command. Troops from both organizations fought together.

As I said, the Santa Clara attack was led by Commander Che Guevara. All the columns of the July 26 Movement and the Directorate participated with concrete tasks: one to take Squadron 31, another unit to attack the armored train, another unit to the jail. The action was carried out with these concrete tasks.

You could call this a collective command. But no one disputed Che's leadership. No one challenged his decisions. Everyone was in agreement. Not "This is yours, that's mine." There was none of that. There was great unity.

Without this unity, the revolution would not have been possible. Such unity has been lacking in some other revolutions, in some other movements that are full of bickering and disagreement.

3. Che Guevara later wrote that when his column reached the Escambray, "they were greeted by an unusual letter. It was signed by Commander Carreras, and it stated that the column of the revolutionary army under my command was prohibited from entering the Escambray without a clear explanation of what we were doing there." Guevara, *Episodes of the Cuban Revolutionary War 1956–58*, p. 393.

The only ones who didn't agree to Che's leadership were those in the Second National Front of the Escambray. The majority of them, or many of them, later became bandits or abandoned the country.

'Remove the rope.
That's what the revolution
was going to do.'

Víctor Dreke addresses rally sponsored by Revolutionary Directorate in Sagua la Grande, November 27, 1959, commemorating execution of eight medical students by Spanish colonial regime in 1871.

After the victory

As the Rebel Army advanced both in Las Villas and Oriente provinces in late 1958, Washington and its allies among the propertied families of Cuba began seeking a formula to forestall a revolutionary victory. On January 1, 1959, with Batista in flight, the defenders of the old order attempted to maintain a government compliant to U.S. interests, announcing a new military regime to replace the dictator.

Fidel Castro responded by calling for a nationwide general strike. The popular masses throughout the island answered the call, pouring into the streets. The attempt to prevent the Rebel Army from taking power was quickly defeated.

With the establishment of the new revolutionary government, the Rebel Army and July 26 Movement immediately began implementing the program around which they had been organizing peasants, workers, and young people from the outset of the struggle. One of the first measures, with broad backing among the Cuban people, was to put on trial, before revolutionary tribunals, several hundred of the worst thugs who had acted as torturers and murderers for the Batista regime. During its first months, the new government also slashed the exorbitant electricity and phone rates that working people paid to the U.S.-owned utility monopolies.

In the opening months of 1959 the government declared illegal the multiple forms of state-sanctioned racial discrimination against blacks. In March discrimination in employment was barred. Over the next several weeks, all stores, shops, and other public facilities including the beaches were declared open to blacks. Rebel Army soldiers and militia members enforced these new measures on the spot, and any facility refusing to abide by them could be shut down forthwith.

The most deep-going measure of the first year of the revolution was the agrarian reform law of May 17, which set a limit of 1,000 acres on individual landholdings. Implementation of the law resulted in the confiscation of the vast estates in Cuba—many of them owned by wealthy U.S. families or by corporations they controlled. These lands passed into the hands of the new government. The law granted share-croppers, tenant farmers, and squatters title to the land they tilled. Some 100,000 peasant families received deeds.

The agrarian reform marked a watershed for bourgeois forces. The Rebel Army–led revolutionary government, they realized, was serious about implementing a program in the interests of the vast majority of Cubans. It could not be bought off, threatened, or diverted. These moneyed interests accelerated their efforts to overthrow the government. Washington too decided the revolutionary leadership had to go and increasingly took steps to implement a course to crush the revolution's supporters, a course that remains in place today, more than forty years later.

The agrarian reform also speeded up the class polarization within the government. Bourgeois forces who had accepted posts—including José Miró Cardona, the first prime minister, and Felipe Pazos, head of the national bank—left Cuba and joined up with the counterrevolution.

From August through October 1960, working people in Cuba responded to the escalation of the U.S. rulers' armed assaults and economic sabotage by carrying out mass mobilizations to enforce the nationalization of the holdings of the major U.S.-owned companies. The expropriation of large Cuban-owned holdings followed.

During this period the Rebel Army, drawing on deep popular support for the revolutionary measures, increased its size, combat readiness, and professionalism. Simultaneously, Cuban working people demonstrated their determination to defend the revolution by flocking to the ranks of the Revolutionary National Militia.

■

WATERS: In January 1959 cadres of the Rebel Army suddenly found yourselves at the head of millions of Cubans more and more determined to transform the country from top to bottom. You began taking on responsibilities you previously would never have imagined.

What were you yourself doing during this initial period?

DREKE: At the triumph of the revolution, I held the rank of captain in the Rebel Army. At that time the top ranks were commander and then captain.

First I was a prosecutor for the revolutionary tribunal. Then I was a battalion chief in the Western Tactical Force.

The Tactical Force was created in May 1959. On May 20 we left Havana on foot with two battalions, headed for Pinar del Río. One went to Guanito and the other to Los Remates de Guane, toward the far end of Pinar del Río. The chief of this Tactical Force in the west was Commander Pinares, who later died in Bolivia with Che, and I was head of G Company and second in command of the 2nd Battalion.

The objective of this operation was to toughen up some compañeros who had joined the revolution in its last days. As we would take a city in the closing months of 1958, new compañeros would join our ranks. And some people hopped on the bandwagon following the triumph, trying to pass themselves off as combatants.

Our task was to identify the people capable of making the effort and then do careful work to train them. Because not everybody could physically withstand a march of hours and hours and hours—with little food, eating in camp, and hard work. They couldn't take it. So this allowed us to do a bit of weeding out. What remained of this Tactical Force was divided into three armies: Western, Central, and Eastern.

When the Western Tactical Force made this trip through the Pinar del Río mountains in May, we had already heard news that the notorious Corporal Luis Lara had risen in revolt there, but we didn't see anything. The trip also made it possible for me to get familiar with Pinar del Río, since the Rebel Army hadn't made it there during the war.

After I returned, Camilo [Cienfuegos], Rebel Army chief of

staff, sent me to Sagua, as head of Squadron 35. At that time we had military squadrons for every region of the country.

Why did they name me chief of this squadron? Well, after the triumph of the revolution there were internal divisions in Sagua, and some problems surfaced among those in charge of the garrison. You'll remember, the Rebel Army didn't get to Sagua before the victory; we got there afterwards. And among those in the Sagua garrison were some people who weren't the best revolutionaries. The same thing happened in other places. These people had taken over and made themselves captains. As a result, some people from Sagua began to voice their complaints very loudly. It was a big mess, a scandal, causing political confusion.

Divisions had grown up between those who had been combatants on April 9 and those who hadn't.[1] This is explained in a speech Camilo gave in Sagua la Grande—it's printed in William Gálvez's book, *Camilo: Señor de la vanguardia* [Camilo: man of the vanguard]—where he read the riot act to people in Sagua for those divisions. And Camilo decided right then and there to name me chief of the Sagua squadron, since I'm from Sagua and knew the compañeros there.

That's why I spent some time in Sagua. Later, I was squadron chief in Cruces, which is also in Las Villas. I went there because of a very difficult racial problem that had to be dealt with.

There had been a dance in the park in Cruces shortly after the victory. As had been the longtime custom in this town, a rope was put up to divide the whites from the blacks—blacks on one side, whites on the other. This time, however, there was a big reaction, first of all from the squadron chief in Cruces, Captain Melquíades García. He was a compañero who was white, a fighter of the Rebel Army, who was highly regarded by all of us

1. On April 9, 1958, the July 26 Movement called a general strike throughout Cuba. Announced without adequate preparation, the strike failed. In response, the Batista forces stepped up repression, and a number of July 26 Movement members were arrested or killed.

as a leader. And for the rebels, white and black were one and the same.

That night in Cruces, this Rebel Army captain removed the rope, and whites and blacks mixed together. Of course a big row developed. Some whites didn't like it, and I suppose some blacks didn't either. Some blacks crossed the line, and all hell broke loose.

The next morning I was summoned to the regimental squadron. I was to report to Félix Torres, inspector general of the regiment. I was taken to a meeting with the squadron chiefs—all of us were there—at which the Cruces events were reported. They described what had happened—the Rebel Army wanting unity among whites, blacks, everyone.

They decided to name a new chief in Cruces. Compañero Melquíades had done what was necessary, since that was what the revolution was going to do: remove the rope. But there had been a row. In fact, there were even leaders of the July 26 Movement in Cruces who had protested because we took down the rope.

"Dreke, you're squadron chief," they told me.

"If they treat blacks that way," I said to myself, "why are they sending *me*?"

Melquíades and I replaced each other. He was named head of Squadron 35 in Sagua, and I became head of Squadron 32 in Cruces. At that time you moved in a matter of hours. It's possible that in the two hours we've spent here talking, I could have been squadron chief in three different places!

"You go here," and then, "No, you go there. You go somewhere else. Get your stuff and go." No one could keep track. That's how it was in those days, a revolutionary whirlwind.

Well, I got to Cruces and introduced myself to the local authorities. They treated me politely. We greeted each other. And then it was explained that I was the new squadron chief.

The first thing I did was go for a walk in the afternoon, passing through the streets, unarmed, to talk to people there. I didn't carry my revolver.

Anyway, I didn't have any problems in Cruces. With the advance of the revolution, that type of racial discrimination has disappeared from our country.

WATERS: What else were you involved in?

DREKE: I was in Sagua as head of Zone Number 4, which was an operational zone encompassing Sagua and Corralillo.

Why was that zone important in 1959–60? Because that was one of the areas where large numbers of weapons drops for the counterrevolutionary groups were made, together with infiltrations through Panchita Beach, Ubero Beach, Carahatas, and all those places. This was due to the characteristics of the Sagua area. There were some large landowners in the area, people who still had great economic power at that time. And it was by the coast.

I was given this mission, head of Zone 4. I worked there until January 13, 1960. Then I went to head up a militia training school in Hatillo,[2] where we prepared compañeros for militia duty in the Escambray clean-up, mainly *milicianos* from Las Villas.

---

2. There was also a school in La Campana, which trained the first militias who defended the region.

'Rifles for the cooks.
Rifles for the teachers.
Rifles for everyone.'

GRANMA

Commander Juan Almeida Bosque (facing camera), then vice minister of the Revolutionary Armed Forces, awarding a unit of the Lucha Contra Bandidos forces with its LCB combat banner.

'Lucha Contra Bandidos' in the Escambray

In 1959–60 the new Cuban power, at the same time inspiring and responding to a rising mass movement, implemented more and more measures in the interests of workers and farmers. As the revolution deepened, the capitalists and landlords and their retainers, with the encouragement and growing support of Washington, sought to overthrow the new government and return themselves to power, restoring their lost property and privileges.

They organized and armed counterrevolutionary bands throughout Cuba. In the cities they began a campaign of arson and sabotage, setting fire to department stores and factories. Well over a hundred Cubans were killed in these terrorist attacks in the first years.

In the rural areas the armed counterrevolutionary groups increasingly became centered in the Escambray mountains of central Cuba. By 1960 dozens of such bands—known in Cuba as simply *los bandidos,* the bandits—were carrying out assassinations and sabotage actions, burning sugarcane fields, and attacking centers of production.

Singled out as special targets were the thousands of teenage literacy brigade volunteers who fanned out across the countryside in early 1961 to teach peasants and workers to read and write, effectively eliminating illiteracy in Cuba by the end of the year. The particularly brutal murder of nineteen-year-old literacy volunteer Conrado Benítez and peasant Eliodoro Rodríguez Linares in January 1961 gave fresh impetus to the massive militia mobilization that was the heart of the first *limpia,* as Cubans called the clean-up operation to eliminate *los bandidos*.

Leaders of the counterrevolutionary bands included men who had at one time taken part in the anti-Batista struggle, as well as others who had either supported Batista or had played no role during the revolutionary war. In the pages that follow, Dreke describes a number of these individuals.

The bandits were armed, supplied, and directed by Washington, which accelerated its aggressive course. In the preparations for what became the 1961 Bay of Pigs invasion, the U.S. administrations of Dwight D. Eisenhower and John F. Kennedy planned for these groups to play an important support role in the aggression. But the Rebel Army and Revolutionary National Militia took decisive action in late 1960 and early 1961 to eliminate that threat.

On April 17, 1961, an expeditionary force of 1,500 Cuban mercenaries—organized, financed, and deployed by Washington—invaded Cuba at the Bay of Pigs on the southern coast. The counterrevolutionaries aimed to spark an antigovernment uprising while holding a beachhead on Cuban territory long enough to install a provisional government already formed in the United States that would appeal for Washington's support and for direct military intervention. In less than seventy-two hours of intense combat, however, the mercenaries were defeated by Cuba's militias, Revolutionary Armed Forces, Revolutionary Air Force, and Revolutionary National Police. On April 19 the remaining invaders were captured at Playa Girón (Girón Beach), which is the name Cubans use to designate the battle.

Víctor Dreke led the two companies from the 117th Battalion that headed to Playa Girón coming in from the village of Yaguaramas to the east. He was wounded in combat.

Another blow to the bandits in the Escambray and their sponsors and armorers in Washington came in October 1963, with the second agrarian reform. This revolutionary measure confiscated landholdings in excess of 165 acres from the remaining 10,000 capitalist farmers, bringing property relations on the land in line with those already established through the expropriation of capitalist industry in the latter half of 1960.

By the end of 1964, as Dreke describes, the fight against the bandits—*la lucha contra bandidos*—had largely been won. In a mop-up operation, the last groups of bandits were eliminated in 1965.

This history of the revolutionary struggle in the Escambray was brought to life in 1999 for new generations of young people in Cuba.

That year eight organizations, representing the majority of the population, joined together to file suit in the Provincial People's Court of the City of Havana to demand that Washington be compelled to pay damages for the human consequences of its forty-year ongoing effort to overthrow the Cuban Revolution. The court hearings in *The People of Cuba v. the U.S. Government* included scores of witnesses giving firsthand testimony detailing U.S. crimes against the Cuban people—thousands of deaths and billions of dollars in physical destruction. The court ruled on November 2, 1999, handing down damages against Washington of $181 billion for the human cost of these crimes.

Witnesses gave testimony in court that in the Escambray, between 1960 and 1965, the bandits were responsible for the deaths of 549 Cubans.

They also pointed out how the fight to defeat the bandits helped mobilize the power of Cuba's workers and farmers during those years, thus strengthening the Cuban Revolution for the challenges to come.

■

WATERS: Outside Cuba, the fight against the counterrevolutionary bands in the Escambray in the first half of the 1960s is a little-known chapter of the revolution. Yet it's one of the decisive battles that molded the revolution. Knowing something about that struggle also helps explain why for more than forty years Washington has underestimated the strength of the revolution. And why, in spite of their concerted military, economic, and political efforts, the U.S. rulers have been unable to crush it.

Who were the bandits? Where did they come from?

DREKE: When we were talking about the war of liberation, I mentioned a number of individuals who had participated in the revolutionary struggle who were in fact adventurers. There were others who were simply opportunist self-seekers, individuals out to grab power, who believed when the revolution triumphed they would trade places with the thieves who had been in control. They would trade places with the brothel owners and become the new owners of the brothels, prostitutes and all.

Early on in the struggle, these people tried to fan the political differences and take advantage of them. As you know, in Cuba there were various revolutionary organizations in the struggle, and some of those people tried to use the divisions flowing from that fact.

Take Evelio Duque, for instance. At the time of the revolutionary war, Duque had been in contact with the Revolutionary Directorate. Even though he was of peasant origin, he had nothing in common with our peasants—our *guajiros*—who in general are good people, noble and friendly people. He was the opposite.

After the revolution's victory, Duque was one of those who tried to recruit to the counterrevolution other compañeros he knew who had fought in the struggle. He tried to divide the different organizations that had fought side by side—organizations that had accepted the leadership of Fidel and Che and whose unity contributed to the revolution's triumph. That's what Evelio Duque tried to do.

There was Eloy Gutiérrez Menoyo, who had also been in the struggle and had betrayed the revolution from the beginning. His first betrayal was leading the split that resulted in the expulsion of the Second National Front of the Escambray. We talked about that earlier. And he continued betraying.

There was William Morgan, the American, who was also part of the Second Front. He was another one who took up arms against the revolution.

There was Plinio Prieto, who was from the Authentic Organization, the group of Aureliano Sánchez Arango and Prío Socarrás. They didn't want to hear anything about revolution.

There was Sinesio Walsh, who was from the July 26 Movement but didn't have anything to do with its principles.

In other words, these are people who belonged to a revolutionary organization, if the July 26 or Revolutionary Directorate armbands and other symbols they had worn were taken at face value. But deep down they didn't answer to either of those two revolutionary organizations, nor to the Popular Socialist Party. They were traitors in waiting, adventurers who wanted to grab power, to be able to keep committing abuses and keep stealing.

WATERS: Why did the Escambray mountains become a center for these counterrevolutionary forces? What was going on in the Escambray?

DREKE: In Cuba at the triumph of the revolution there were a half million illiterates, and there were another half million who were only semiliterate. That was the concrete situation. If one were to go to Pinar del Río or to the Escambray the situation was terrible. There was no electricity, no running water—what little water there was came from wells. There were no stores. There were few radios, since you couldn't even receive radio signals throughout much of these mountainous areas. All this made the enemy's job easier.

From the time of the revolutionary war, nearly all these individuals I've talked about—who would eventually become counterrevolutionaries—were concentrated in the Escambray. They worked on some peasants and managed to recruit a few. At the same time, they also committed abuses in the areas where they functioned. They murdered peasants, they raped peasant women. They burned down schools and homes. So the peasants were terrorized; they were deathly afraid of the counterrevolutionaries. Some peasants joined them consciously, of course, but others joined out of fear. This is how the counterrevolutionary movement was built.

One of their first actions was the attempt to take Trinidad and destroy the revolution. I'm referring to the attempted landing organized by Dominican President Trujillo.[1]

There were others who didn't commit murders—such as

---

1. In August 1959, a plane bearing armed counterrevolutionaries organized by the dictatorship of Rafael Trujillo in the Dominican Republic was captured after landing at the airport of Trinidad in south-central Cuba. The

Luis Vargas, to give you a concrete example. Vargas had always been a bandit who devoted himself full time to robbery. He stole here; he stole there; he rustled cattle; he had five or ten wives. Luis Vargas had always been in armed rebellion in the Escambray, until finally we put an end to the notorious Luis Vargas.

In some other parts of Las Villas province, in the Sagua-Corralillos eastern region, there were persons such as Benito Campos and his son Martí, the "Campitos." These people and others like them had been characterized by the same immorality and the same unwillingness to do battle with the dictator's army. These were people who simply wanted to become the new millionaires.

WATERS: In several of Fidel's speeches during 1962 he spoke of problems in the application and implementation of the Agrarian Reform in Matanzas and the Escambray. He pointed out that this political situation was responsible for the fact that the bandits gained some influence among layers of the peasants.

DREKE: Yes, that's true. At the beginning no authentic agrarian reform was carried out in the Escambray. Why was this? Because those in charge of the agrarian reform in Trinidad and Sancti Spíritus weren't in fact revolutionaries.

One of those in charge of the agrarian reform there, for example, was the counterrevolutionary Evelio Duque who I just mentioned. Duque headed up INRA in Sancti Spíritus, and he removed the compañeros who were revolutionaries from the agrarian reform and its leadership. He removed people like Commander Julio Castillo, a revolutionary who was highly re-

plane was the same one used by Fulgencio Batista to flee Cuba seven months earlier.

The counterrevolutionaries belonged to the Anti-Communist Legion of the Caribbean, which included individuals from various countries, among them a large number of Cubans, several of whom had been officers in Batista's army. In the fighting two of the counterrevolutionaries were killed and a number were taken prisoner; two Cuban defenders of the revolution were also killed and nine wounded.

garded in Sancti Spíritus. Then Duque recruited others who, like himself, weren't revolutionaries.

What did Duque do? He committed a series of injustices. He expropriated land that shouldn't have been taken. Or else he extorted money in exchange for not expropriating someone's land.

So the agrarian reform wasn't implemented as the commander in chief and the revolutionary leadership had laid out in the Agrarian Reform Law. Nor as Che and the compañeros of the Directorate had done during the war.[2]

One of those in charge of the agrarian reform there was William Morgan, who devised a plan called Rana Toro [bullfrog]. Rana Toro was a scheme to bring in weapons and hide them in Charco Azul, in order to prepare an uprising by the bandits. This same William Morgan, who had murdered peasants and raped women during the war in the zone where the Second National Front of the Escambray operated, was preparing the conditions for an uprising.

Another one of these individuals was the notorious Jesús Carreras, who had also been a leader of the Second Front.

In fairness, it's important to state that while the Second Front was dominated by a group of criminals and traitors, some young revolutionaries also found their way into its ranks. They were victims of those people, and they're here with the revolution today. The revolution hasn't tossed them off, because not everybody in the Second Front was the same. To say otherwise would be illogical and untrue. There were exceptions. There were also peasants who took up arms and later put them back down and left the bandits, after realizing they had made a mistake.

But the leadership of the Second Front did have characteristics that made them act this way. And later they united with others who were traitors, embezzlers, and rapists. All those

2. See Guevara's "Military Order number 1" in Las Villas, printed in *Episodes of the Cuban Revolutionary War*, pp. 380–81.

of that ilk got together. Some came from the Directorate, others from the July 26 Movement, some from other places, and they all joined together with the worst elements of the Second Front.

It's also true that at first the necessary attention wasn't paid to the Escambray. The most qualified persons were not utilized there, and we didn't stay on top of things. We should have designated those in charge of major responsibilities. That's my personal opinion.

Already in 1959 there were bandits there. I was in a position to know, since, along with other compañeros, I participated in various operations in the Escambray.

The enemies of the revolution had already studied the situation, and they realized the Escambray would be the best spot for them. There were problems within the revolutionary ranks, and our work there was the weakest.

Some bandits had posts initially.

Osvaldo Ramírez, the murderer and traitor, was squadron chief of the Caracusey garrison in Trinidad. And the first thing he did was to run the peasants off their farms and take away their land. You must know what that meant. Captain San Luis, who was squadron chief in Trinidad and later became a combatant in Che's unit in Bolivia, had to go there and kick him out. That's why Osvaldo was dismissed. But it was an error to let Osvaldo take the position there as squadron chief in the first place.

Sinesio Walsh—the same person I talked of earlier—was named squadron chief in Cruces.

Benito Campos—"Campito"—was chief in the Corralillo zone, where he committed atrocities.

The conscious revolutionaries at that time were not yet Marxists or Leninists—and I'm not just speaking about myself—but at least we wanted a revolution. We wanted to prevent the bourgeoisie from returning to power. We wanted the poor to be in charge. We wanted racial equality. That's what we were then.

But the fact is we gave the Escambray to the bandits as a gift during the first stage. That has to be said.

Top: On January 15, 1953, a demonstration of university students in Havana against the dictatorship of Fulgencio Batista is attacked by police. On the ground is Rubén Batista, who has just been shot. He died from his wounds several weeks later—the first student martyr in the fight against the tyranny. **Bottom:** Fidel Castro being interrogated in captivity after leading the July 26, 1953, attack on the Moncada garrison in Santiago de Cuba.

"Fidel Castro took up arms against Batista. That made us more confident about taking the road of revolutionary struggle."

"We protested because we believed Batista was bad, but we didn't have a clear idea of what we hoped to accomplish."

COURTESY VÍCTOR DREKE   MIL FOTOS CUBA→

Above: Members of the Youth Movement of the Third Regional Workers Federation in Sagua la Grande commemorate the twenty-first anniversary of the assassination of Antonio Guiteras, May 8, 1956. Víctor Dreke is squatting at left. The action was subsequently broken up by the police. **Inset**: Antonio Guiteras, a leader of the 1933 revolutionary upsurge in Cuba. **Facing page, top**: Dreke helped organize support for the December 1955 nationwide strike by 200,000 sugar workers to protest government move to lower wages; a number of towns in Las Villas, where the strike was centered, were virtually taken over by the workers and their supporters. **Bottom**: Dreke joined other Cuban youth in protesting the U.S.-organized overthrow of the government of Jacobo Arbenz in Guatemala, June 1954. In photo, peasants are rounded up and brought to the central police station in Guatemala City for opposing the coup, July 1954.

"Without the unity of the revolutionary forces, victory would not have been possible."

Above: Leaders of units of July 26 Movement and Revolutionary Directorate at Directorate's camp at Dos Arroyos. Standing: Jorge Martín, Humberto Castelló, Faure Chomón, René Rodríguez, Rolando Cubela, Che Guevara, Ramiro Valdés. Kneeling at left, José Moleón, Raúl Nieves. **Facing page, top:** Peasant family in the Escambray mountains, close to Trinidad, around the time of the revolution. They are standing in front of their thatch-roof hut typical of housing in rural areas of Cuba before 1959. **Center right:** Raúl Castro addresses Congress of Peasants in Arms organized by Rebel Army's Second Eastern Front in Oriente, September 21, 1958.

Revolutionary Directorate combatants in the Escambray, 1958: **Bottom,** Tony Santiago and Faure Chomón, the commander of the Directorate column, at steering wheel. **Center left,** Ramón González Coro (Mongo), facing camera, and Raúl López Pardo (Raulín).

ANTONIO NÚÑEZ JIMÉNEZ

COURTESY VÍCTOR DREKE

BOHEMIA

"In Santa Clara the entire people came out in the streets and joined us. We saw the incipient militias of the revolution."

ANTONIO NÚÑEZ JIMÉNEZ

Above: During the battle of Santa Clara, Cubans parked their cars in the middle of the streets to impede the dictatorship's tanks. **Facing page, top left:** Che Guevara outside the army garrison in Santa Clara, January 1, 1959. **Top right:** A *miliciano* in Santa Clara poses with a Molotov cocktail after the victory. **Bottom:** Headquarters of Squadron 31 following army's surrender, January 1, 1959.

The Freedom Caravan:
The main columns of
the Rebel Army enter
Havana, January 8,
1959. Standing in jeep,
wearing hat, is Camilo
Cienfuegos.

GRANMA

"At that time you moved in a matter of hours. No one could keep track. It was a revolutionary whirlwind."

Above: A half million peasants from all over Cuba were organized to come to Havana, July 26, 1959, many for the first time in their lives. The peasants were housed by working people of the city. **Facing page, top:** On March 4, 1960, *La Coubre,* a French ship carrying Belgian munitions for the workers militias, was blown up in Havana harbor. The arms had been purchased with contributions by the Cuban people. The terrorist act killed 95 people. **Center:** Members of Cuba's first workers militias march in Havana's May Day parade in 1959. **Bottom:** Members of 6th Company of 2nd Infantry Battalion of the Rebel Army's Western Tactical Force on training exercises, climbing the highest mountain in Pinar del Río in early 1959. Víctor Dreke is standing, second from left.

"The Rebel Army was the people— it was the people in uniform."

Top left: Militia members in the Escambray learning to read and write, 1961. **Top right:** Peasant family being taught by literacy brigade member, 1961. A photo of Camilo Cienfuegos hangs on the wall. **Above:** Conrado Benítez, 19-year-old literacy volunteer murdered by counterrevolutionary bands, January 1961. **Bottom left:** Peasant women cleaning rice as they prepare lunch for militia members fighting counterrevolutionary bands.

> **"Entire battalions of peasant militias from the Escambray were formed. What the enemy thought would be a den of thieves became a bulwark of the revolution."**

Clockwise from below: Rebel Army commander Raúl Menéndez Tomassevich, head of the LCB, interrogating a captured bandit. Sinesio Walsh, leader of one of the first counterrevolutionary bands, captured in 1960. Bodies of peasants murdered by counterrevolutionaries being exhumed, March 1961.

From the youngest to the oldest militia members in the Escambray: Fourteen-year-old combatant on horse, March 1961. Sixty-five-year-old Andrés Aguiar, at right. Militia members in Escambray in action, March 1961.

OPT INVS G-2
SINESIO WALSH RIOS
ALZADO SIERRA DEL ESCAMBRAY

0 5 8 1 1

GRANMA

"Our troops never abused a single prisoner, even though they had committed a great many murders, and we hated them."

GRANMA

Above: Working people of Trinidad join funeral procession for paper workers murdered by counterrevolutionaries on their way home from work, December 1963. **Left:** A few of the U.S.-supplied weapons captured from bandits.

"Struggles against U.S. imperialism were advancing outside Cuba, too. Around the world there was an escalation of national liberation struggles to throw off colonialism and imperialist domination. This was especially true in Africa."

Above: Thousands of Congolese protest Belgian colonial rule in Léopoldville, January 1959. The actions began when Belgian troops broke up an "unauthorized" meeting discussing independence. Thousands of Congolese responded by throwing up barricades against the machine guns of the colonial forces, who killed more than forty. **Top right:** Police attack women anti-apartheid demonstrators in Durban, South Africa, 1959. **Center, right:** Rally in Algeria to support struggle for independence from France, early 1960s. **Center, left:** Vietnamese anti-aircraft gunners defending their country against U.S. air attacks, mid-1960s. **Bottom:** Dominicans confront U.S. invasion forces, 1965.

EDITORIAL CIENCIAS SOCIALES

"The revolution's position has been to support liberation movements by all peoples on all continents."

Above: Patrice Lumumba, prime minister of the Congo and leader of the country's liberation struggle, at June 1960 independence ceremony where he denounced "the humiliating slavery imposed on us" by Belgian imperialism. Lumumba was overthrown in a U.S.- and Belgian-backed coup in September 1960 and murdered in January 1961. **Facing page, top:** Right to left, Che Guevara, José María Martínez Tamayo (Papi), and Rogelio Olivia in the Congo, 1965. **Center, left:** Mercenary belonging to imperialist-organized forces, standing over body of slain Congolese fighter, 1964. **Center, right:** Che Guevara, holding child, with Congolese fighter, 1965. **Bottom:** Boat carrying retreating Cuban combatants from the Congo to Tanzania, November 1965.

"The experience we gained in the Congo made it possible for us to do what we did to aid the liberation struggles in Guinea-Bissau, Angola, and other places."

Above: Amilcar Cabral, left, leader of the national liberation movement in Portuguese colonial-ruled Guinea-Bissau and Cape Verde, with Víctor Dreke, head of Cuba's military mission in Guinea-Bissau, 1967.

Top: Cuban combatants from the military mission in Guinea-Bissau, 1967. Left to right: Juan Gómez, Víctor Dreke, Reynaldo Batista, Cintra Capote. **Center**: Víctor Dreke with Conchita Dubois in Guinea-Bissau, 1967, where she was assigned to military intelligence. Women took other internationalist assignments in Africa, but prior to Cuba's thirteen-year military mission in Angola, Dubois was the only Cuban woman to serve in a combat unit there. **Bottom**: Cuban women's antiaircraft artillery and antitank unit in Angola, 1988.

T.J. FIGUEROA/MILITANT

OROZCO/JUVENTUD REBELDE

MARY-ALICE WATERS/MILITANT

"Cuba and Africa have influenced each other deeply."

Top: Cuban volunteer doctors in South Africa, 2000. Center: First contingent of Che Guevara Internationalist Teachers Detachment returns to Cuba from Angola, 1979. Bottom: African National Congress president Nelson Mandela and Fidel Castro, at rally in Matanzas, Cuba, July 26, 1991.

When the first clean-up operation began in 1960, when the army arrived, when Fidel arrived, the peasants responded, and entire battalions of peasant militias from the Escambray were formed. The peasants asked for weapons and they defended the Escambray. So what the enemy thought was going to be a den of thieves was, by determined revolutionary combat, turned into a bulwark of the revolution.

MADRID: In October 1963 the Second Agrarian Reform was decreed and implemented, eliminating one of the key social bases of the counterrevolutionary bands, that of the remaining capitalist farmers.

What impact did this law have on the struggle against the bandits?

DREKE: The Second Agrarian Reform helped. The wealthy landowners bought off those people. Many gave them support. But that's jumping ahead.

We did a number of things in the Escambray. At one point we had to seize a lot of property. I participated in this, together with people from the Escambray. We confiscated all the cars belonging to the counterrevolutionaries, all the *timbiriches*—that's what we call the tiny bodegas, or stores—that belonged to those who consciously assisted the bandits. Those who helped the bandits, protecting them, hiding them, and providing them with supplies, food, and other items. Some did so because they were forced to by the bandits. It was a little of both.

One night the army went in—and when I say "army," I mean the people's militias, the armed people, made up of the peasants themselves—and we confiscated all those things. It was a lightning operation. And by daybreak the bandits had nothing. They were left without supplies. They were left without a rear guard. Later they put one back together, but we put them in that situation for several months.

It was necessary to deepen the revolution's political work in the Escambray. That required making changes there in the leadership of the party, of the armed forces, of everything. The commander in chief; the minister of defense, Raúl; and Almeida, who had been named head of the Central Army—all of them were part of this. So the political and ideological work was turned around.

WATERS: The troops, the militia who were decisive in defeating the bands—were they all volunteers? I'm thinking of Nicaragua, where there were differences among the Sandinistas over whether to fight the U.S.-organized contra forces with volunteers or draftees. The Sandinista leadership eventually decided on a draft, and the revolution's enemies used that to gain support.

DREKE: In our case they were volunteers.

In the first clean-up operation 50,000 combatants participated, most of them from Havana province. The militias executed a massive encirclement of the Escambray.

WATERS: When was this?

DREKE: The first clean-up operation in the Escambray ran from the end of 1960 through the first months of 1961. But we had to withdraw our troops with a few bands still remaining. And then in April came Playa Girón.

We withdrew our troops early on in 1961 because they had already been mobilized for months. They were workers and peasants who had voluntarily left their workplaces and were absent from their jobs. Since they were taking part in the cleanup operation, they weren't producing. It's important to remember that the enemy used the counterrevolutionary bands in the Escambray to try to drain the resources of the fledgling revolution, which was fighting to resolve the country's economic problems.

Most militia volunteers weren't getting paid anything. For those who had jobs, their factories and workplaces continued to pay their wages to their families. But most were youth in their teens who had never been part of the work force. Only some years later, as an "incentive," to use the language of today, did we start giving 25 pesos a month to young *milicianos* who didn't hold regular jobs.

All of them were there by their own choice. They were the volunteer forces of the people.

Tens of thousands of militiamen took part. How were we able to mobilize them? Because of acts like the murder of literacy volunteers, among them Conrado Benítez and Manuel Ascunce,[3] as well as innocent peasant women and children—and all the other crimes the bandits had committed: burning down schools, rapes, robberies. The people rose up in indignation over these savage deeds.

MADRID: How important was the first clean-up operation in the Escambray to ensuring the defeat of the invasion at Girón?

DREKE: It was very important. Let me explain why.

These bandits were dependent on imperialism. We can't look at the bandits in isolation, on their own, as just some group of crazies who took up arms. No, no, no. This was organized. They were being organized as a fifth column to back an invasion by the United States. An important mission was assigned to these bandits by Washington.[4]

3. Conrado Benítez, a nineteen-year-old literacy volunteer, was murdered by a counterrevolutionary band in the Escambray January 5, 1961, along with a peasant, Eliodoro Rodríguez Linares. Manuel Ascunce, a sixteen-year-old literacy volunteer, was murdered by counterrevolutionaries in the Escambray November 26, 1961, together with Pedro Lantigua, a peasant he was teaching to read and write.

   Prior to the revolution, 23.6 percent of the Cuban population was illiterate. In the countryside illiteracy reached 41 percent, and if those who were semiliterate are included, the figure was over 80 percent. From late 1960 through the end of 1961 the revolutionary government organized a national campaign to teach one million Cubans to read and write. Central to this effort was the mobilization of 100,000 young people to go to the countryside, where they lived with peasants they were teaching. As a result of this drive, Cuba eliminated illiteracy. The residual illiteracy rate—those with learning disabilities and mental or physical impairments that prevented them from being taught—was 3.9 percent at the end of the successful campaign.

4. This mission was described in a presidential briefing paper from August 1960, quoted by then CIA Inspector General Lyman Kirkpatrick in a balance sheet of the defeated Bay of Pigs invasion written in October 1961, but released only in 1998. The August 1960 Eisenhower administration memo said: "The initial phase of paramilitary operations envisages the development, support and guidance of dissident groups in three areas of Cuba: Pinar

At the time of the first clean-up, the mission for which the bandits were being prepared was to attack and seize the main towns when the invasion came—Trinidad and all those little towns there—and to take the highways. In addition, within the cities it was expected that organized counterrevolutionaries would take up arms when the moment came.

In other words, all this was being directed by imperialism.

What happened?

The commander in chief, Fidel, led the process of eliminating the bands prior to Girón. The murder and harassment of peasants had to be stopped. What's more, we knew an attack was coming. There had already been various types of sabotage actions by the bandits in different regions. For example, near Trinidad they blew up fuel tanks.

We made the effort to rapidly clean up the Escambray, so we wouldn't face a fifth column already armed and trained.

When the landing came at Girón, very few of the bandits remained. They were in flight. They were in hiding. They controlled nothing. This was part of defeating the U.S. invasion plan. The invaders were left without a rear guard.

In the cities State Security immediately grabbed them all. This included some people we thought were counterrevolutionaries but weren't. Because at that time, you couldn't say anything against the revolution. You couldn't say, "Damn it's cold and we don't have shelter." You couldn't say that because it would be interpreted as counterrevolutionary. That's the way it was. The question was one of *"Patria o muerte!"* [Homeland or death] Because that was the only way forward.

So there were people we considered counterrevolutionaries

del Rio, Escambray and Sierra Maestra. These groups will be organized for concerted guerrilla action against the regime."

Kirkpatrick also cites a secret White House memo from March 11, 1961—four days prior to the Kennedy administration's decision to switch the proposed invasion from the Escambray region to Playa Girón. The memo reported that the revolutionary government "is making good use of the militia against guerrilla activities and the infiltration of people and hardware."

because of reports and opinions expressed by their neighbors or coworkers. But when the invasion came, they went out into the streets requesting arms to fight.

But the real counterrevolutionaries were neutralized. We tied their feet. They couldn't do anything. The invaders were left with no reserve forces. They believed they had an army awaiting them. But when they arrived they found they had nothing. Their "army" had been crushed.

WATERS: Where were you when the invasion at Girón began?

DREKE: In April 1961 I was head of the Hatillo militia training school, which I mentioned earlier. A session of the school had just ended, and I requested a transfer to Oriente, to the Tactical Force of Oriente in Caney de las Mercedes headed by compañero Armando Acosta. I left very early on the morning of April 17, 1961, the very day of the invasion.

On the way I stopped in Santa Clara to pick up the letter of transfer at the general staff headquarters.

When I got there, I looked around and it was bedlam. There were people coming and going every which way.

"What's happened?" I asked.

"The mercenaries have landed at Girón," someone told me—although I think they said it was the Americans that had landed. At the time I sort of knew where Girón was, but I'd never been there before.

I jumped into the car and headed for Girón. At each town I came to, I'd ask "Where's Girón?" They said it was close to Yaguaramas, so I headed over there.

When I got to Yaguaramas, I witnessed a moving scene. The population of the town was in the street asking for arms and applauding all the combatants as we passed through.

As we went through the area we could hear shots. Canefields were on fire and cars were burning.

I came across a group of militia compañeros from the 117th Battalion. I took command of the battalion and got in touch with compañero René de los Santos at the command post in Yaguaramas. Later that day we clashed with an enemy paratroop unit.

The evening of April 18 the commander in chief gave us instructions that at dawn our artillery would open fire and that our troops were to begin advancing shortly after that, to arrive in Girón at 6:00 p.m. on April 19.

As we were advancing on the 19th, I noticed it was already 4:00 p.m. and we still had quite a ways to go. I hopped in a jeep with two or three compañeros and said, "Let's get to Girón!"

The previous night three tanks had arrived, along with compañero Emilio Aragonés, and they were now accompanying us. But instead of staying with the tanks, which were our protection, the jeep got out in front of the company.

Shortly after 5:00 we fell into an ambush by one of the remaining small enemy groups. As I was aiming my rifle, I was shot in the arm and the leg. The compañeros put me in the jeep and took me to Santa Clara.

Within an hour after I was wounded, our forces took Girón.

WATERS: After the first clean-up operation and the defeat of the U.S.-organized forces at the Bay of Pigs, what was the situation of the bandits? How did they regroup and reorganize?

DREKE: Out of the first clean-up, one group of bandits escaped unharmed and managed to hide. It included Osvaldo Ramírez, Tartabul, and Campito. At a famous gathering of the bandits in July 1961, called the Cicatero meeting, the bands were restructured. The CIA had its hand in this, along with Osvaldo and Evelio Duque, who were together. A dispute eventually erupted between those two over who was going to be in charge. But at this meeting, a new structure was created that involved dividing up the bandits in the Escambray by zone, by area.[5]

In response, we divided up the Escambray into sectors, structuring it the way the bandits had done. We'd received pretty good information from State Security.

---

5. At the July 1961 meeting held in the tiny village of Cicatero, the surviving bandit leaders divided up the Escambray into five zones. By the beginning of 1962, there were some 500 men in 41 bands in Las Villas province, and another 30 groups in the rest of the country.

The three main sectors we set up in the Escambray were Sector A, Sector F, and Sector G. Sector A encompassed Salto de Habanilla, which was a very important area, one of the most mountainous zones of the Escambray. Sector F was in Banao. And Sector G was in Minas Bajas, which is next to the Santa Clara region.

The first headquarters of the Escambray section was set up in Manicaragua. Later it was transferred to Trinidad.

There were additional sectors, as well. Sector B was created in the Yaguajay zone, encompassing Florencia, Tamarindo, Arroyo Blanco, and the zone where the bandit Mario Bravo and those people were. Sector C covered the zone of Rodas, Cartagena, part of Cienfuegos, and Aguada de Pasajeros, where there were also bandits. Sector D covered Sagua-Corralillo. Sector E encompassed Camagüey, Ciego de Avila, and all those places, which were then a single province going up to the border of Oriente province. Those were the main sectors at that time. There were also the Matanzas sectors, which I'm not going to get into right now.

What were the characteristics of the sectors and subsectors?

Each sector had a four-person command: a military head, a political instructor, a chief of information, and a doctor or nurse. Since at that time we didn't have too many doctors, the fourth was often a nurse. In 1961, when the literacy campaign began, we added a teacher, since our soldiers were illiterate and they too were learning how to read and write. Each sector was then divided into zones. With this structure, a more organized and effective stage of the battle began.

In July 1962 the commander in chief and the minister of the Revolutionary Armed Forces created a specialized command, the LCB—Lucha Contra Bandidos [struggle against bandits]. This new command operated in the Escambray, in Las Villas province, and throughout the country.

Those of us assigned to the LCB were the same ones who'd previously participated in pursuing the bandits as members of the Rebel Army and the militias. The command was headed up

MATANZAS PROVINCE

CÁRDENAS
Máximo Gómez
Remco
Colón
Los Arabos
Manguito
Calimete

Rancho Veloz
RAMONA
Quemado de Güines
Maracas
Santo Domingo
San Diego del Valle
La Esperanza

Isabela de Sagua
Sagua la Grande

D

EM LCB

SANTA CLARA

Remedios
Camajuaní
Caibarién

B

BATALLA DE PERALEJO
Aguada de Pasajeros
Rodas
Cruces
Yaguaramas
Abreus

C

CIENFUEGOS
Cumanayagua

MANICARAGUA
Fomento
Cabaiguán
Guayos

ESCAMBRAY

SANCTI SPÍRITUS

Yaguajay
MENESES

A

SANCTI SPÍRITUS

LAS VILLAS PROVINCE

TRINIDAD

Majagua

Organization of LCB section

❏ *Leadership and general staff of the section*
❏ *Units of combat supply and services*
❏ *5 sectors and 30 subsectors*
❏ *6 operational groups*
❏ *100 companies (some were later incorporated into battalions)*
❏ *5 schools*

Territorial division of Lucha Contra Bandidos Central Army July 1962 to July 1965

Objective

Prepare and deploy specialized units in irregular warfare operations aimed at eliminating banditry once and for all and protecting the civilian population and economic, political, and social institutions.

Missions

Plan and direct military operations to capture or annihilate the groups of bandits in the affected zones.

Organize and train the specialized units assigned to carry out this type of struggle. For this, a school should be created in each operational sector.

Carry out a broad and systematic political, ideological, and social effort aimed at raising the level of understanding of the residents of the regions with regard to the justice of the line and principles of our socialist revolution, contributing to the rapid annihilation of the bands and preventing the emergence of new ones.

Protect the civilian population and economic, political, and social centers.

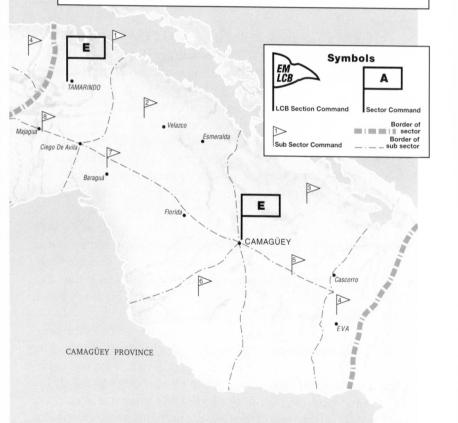

Symbols

EM LCB | LCB Section Command

A | Sector Command

Sub Sector Command

Border of sector

Border of sub sector

TAMARINDO

Majagua

Ciego De Avila

Baraguá

Velazco

Esmeralda

Florida

CAMAGÜEY

Cascorro

EVA

CAMAGÜEY PROVINCE

ORIENTE PROVINCE

by compañero Raúl Menéndez Tomassevich. Previously the fight against the bandits had been directed by Piti Fajardo and then Dermidio Escalona; after Tomassevich it was headed by Osvaldo "Pineo" Lorenzo Castro and then Lizardo Proenza.

I was second in command of the LCB overall and headed the forces in the Escambray sector, an area that includes parts of the present-day provinces of Cienfuegos, Sancti Spíritus, and Villa Clara. At that time these were all part of a single province, Las Villas.

We began operations with information provided by the peasants.

"There's a group of bandits over there," they would tell us.

We'd run out to catch them. Sometimes there would be bandits, sometimes just peasants cutting undergrowth. Other times they'd tell us there were bandits somewhere, and we'd say: "There aren't any bandits there; that's crazy. It's all lies." Then it turned out there really were bandits there. All those things happened during the initial stage of the fight.

We established a very important school in Condado, the Corporals' School. Its purpose was to train leaders of squads and other small units that would be the first troops to clash with the enemy.

A corporal is the immediate superior for a squad. It's a very important rank. Because in a military operation each piece of terrain is covered by a squad, that is, by seven, eight, sometimes ten men. It varied. Seven was the usual figure for us at the time, and there was a leader among these seven men who commanded the group.

So a school was established to prepare these youth for command, since they were peasants, workers, students who had no military background. They hadn't participated in the war of liberation. And the Rebel Army wasn't big enough to fill all the command positions we now needed. We were not even three thousand men in arms at the time the revolution triumphed. But even before, the idea had never been for the Rebel Army to hold all the command positions. Why? Because, as Camilo said, the

Rebel Army was the people—it was the people in uniform.

The situation was the same in the Escambray.

In addition to compañeros already in the Rebel Army, the school included the militia officers, who we referred to as militia lieutenants, to be trained as battalion and company commanders, and so on. There were company-level people, such as Gustavo Castellón—"the Mayaguara Horse"— Julián Morejón, Catalino Olaechea, and others who became quite famous in the struggle against the bandits.

During this new stage, State Security began to play a more important, a more fundamental role than previously. I mentioned earlier that there were places where we lacked information. State Security was now beginning to get organized. Wherever we had a sector there was a State Security group. They worked on their own but they collaborated with us in the LCB.

Furthermore, the party had its own structure in the zone. The Federation of Women, the CDRs, ANAP, and the youth organization were all working in the zone.[6] In other words, the revolutionary organizations were participating together with us throughout the entire battle. The political and ideological work they conducted was very important.

In addition, a series of social measures were taken in the Escambray.

Medical centers were set up throughout the region with doctors from Havana or Santa Clara, and medical supplies were made available to the population. The first doctors to graduate after the victory of the revolution, those who were in medical school at the time of the triumph, were sent to the Escambray. Schools were established, and we provided teachers for them.

We set up the Ana Betancourt School in Havana, where young

6. This is a reference to the Federation of Cuban Women (FMC), the Committees for the Defense of the Revolution (CDR), the National Association of Small Farmers (ANAP), and the Association of Rebel Youth (AJR), which in April 1962 became the Union of Young Communists (UJC).

women from the Escambray came to learn sewing and other skills. They were housed in the mansions abandoned by wealthy owners—some the former landlords of the peasant women. Later they went back to the Escambray to teach the same skills to others.

Plus we established what was called the "Escambray Plan" to develop agriculture in the region. Members of the LCB would help the peasants during the coffee harvests, for example.

Every officer was there with his unit. We were present in the battles, combing the area together with the troops, exchanging fire with the bandits. This is one of the things about our armed forces that allowed us to wipe out the bandits—the personal example of the commanding officers, who were always with their troops in combat.

Along these lines, the compañeros sometimes tell a story about me. I don't remember it, so I don't know if it's true or not. One night, they say, I was asleep in camp. One of the compañeros returning from guard duty didn't recognize who I was and woke me up, saying, "Hey, get me some food." Or "Bring me some water to cook with." Because the commanding officers were right there along with the rest of the men. You were just like everybody else. That's how the struggle against the bandits was.

The commander in chief himself was the first to set the example, on the front lines, firing at the bandits. This was an extremely dangerous time. The death of Fidel would have been very dangerous for the revolution. But as he would say, "We have to set the example." That's the way it is. And besides, Fidel is Fidel, always in the front lines of combat.

Like when there's a hurricane. The commander heads right out there and no one can stop him.[7] That's the way he is. We wish he wouldn't do that, but we love him more for it. It's the same

7. Hurricane Flora slammed into eastern Cuba in October 1963, killing more than a thousand people, destroying 10,000 homes, and severely damaging agricultural production. In the midst of the hurricane, Fidel Castro went to the affected area and became directly involved in the rescue operation.

with Raúl. The minister is our best teacher.

During the early part of this phase of the struggle to eliminate the bandits, these bands murdered many people—because, even though we had this structure set up, it really wasn't operationally strong at first. There'd be a company of 100 men, let's say. But since it had to cover such a vast territory, when the company went here, the bandits would hit you there; when you went there, they'd hit you here. They started burning down stores, murdering literacy brigadistas, and instilling fear among the teachers who were participating in the literacy campaign.

There were moments when we couldn't do anything and that made us so angry. They'd attack some place and we'd arrive and comb the area, catching one or two of them. But the next day they'd be attacking somewhere else.

Later we went on the offensive, but we still didn't have troops mobilized in Manicaragua, where I was.

One morning in 1963 an informant for State Security came and told us there was a group of bandits in Manicaragua, at the entrance to the town. There's a bridge there, as I mentioned earlier. The bandits were led by Porfirio Guillén, who was one of the leaders appointed by Julio Emilio Carretero and Osvaldo Ramírez.

To tell you the truth, I thought the information was false.

"It's a lie," I said.

I was stubborn. But I issued orders to the compañeros, "All right, let's go fire some shots and find out."

But we had a problem. We had hardly any troops right there, just one company, the famous company of the Mayaguara Horse— and part of it was on leave. This company at the time had forty-five men, and sometimes we'd wind up with thirty or so. It wasn't a company of a hundred. And it's not possible to organize an encirclement with thirty-five or forty-five men. The bandits would just slip through.

The bandits were there, moreover, because they were planning to attack Manicaragua. Imagine how embarrassing it would have been if the bandits were to get into Manicaragua, near our headquarters. I thought they were sticking their tongue out at us. I really did.

MADRID: How many bandits were there? Was it a single group?

DREKE: There were eighteen or nineteen bandits hidden there. They were part of a single band, that of Porfirio Guillén. Tartabul was second in command.

We prepared to launch the operation. With whom? With every compañero who could breathe. We got the cooks together. Rifles for the cooks. Rifles for the teachers. Rifles for everyone, including myself of course. And we headed out. We got there and clashed with the bandits.

We captured almost the entire band, among them Guillén. Tartabul escaped, but we caught up with him later. Three of our compañeros were killed.

It was a staggering blow for the bandits.

This was in 1963. It was a moment when they still had some strength. They had been located virtually inside the city itself, since we didn't have the troops to hit them with. They were confident we wouldn't be able to handle them, that they could attack Manicaragua, firing their rifles, and then flee. They weren't trying to capture it, because to do that they would've had to kill us all. But they were confident they could create trouble in Manicaragua, in the city, and then flee.

WATERS: How were the bandits finally defeated?

DREKE: We used different tactics. The encirclements were always done at dawn or in the middle of the night. They couldn't be carried out during the day. You had to march at night in order to surprise the bandits sleeping or eating, or partying, as they did every so often. They would drink a few bottles of rum and we'd surround them sleeping it off.

Above all we marched during bad weather, when it was cold and rainy. Those were the optimal times to operate, since the bandits didn't move. Wherever they got to during the day, they stayed and camped for the night. When they felt secure they would spend two or three days in the same place. Those were moments of maximum opportunity during which a number of members of State Security were able to penetrate the bands. This happened throughout the Escambray.

Later the battalions were mobilized and operational divisions were created.

The LCB battalions didn't operate solely in the Escambray; they moved through various operational zones. We would move a division from one spot to another, to operate in a different area. We would move it toward Sagua; we would move it toward Camagüey, which was a very convulsive region, the Jatibonico region; Sancti Spíritus, where there were many bands, such as the zone Mario Bravo operated in. We would move these units to carry out these operations to root them out.

There's something about the antibandit struggle that I think is important for everyone to understand: Our troops never abused a single prisoner. We never mistreated a single one, even though those prisoners had committed a great many murders, and we hated them. We hated them. That has to be said. Because you saw peasants murdered, women massacred, children orphaned. You never want to hate a human being, of course, but the individuals who did these things had first and last names that we knew.

There were some bandits of whom we'd say, "We must pursue and capture so-and-so at all costs." We were all hardheaded about this, all of us involved in the struggle against the bandits—compañeros like Lizardo Proenza, the last commander of the LCB, who was a great compañero in the struggle against bandits. Tomás[sevich] too. We were all that way. They had to be captured. Because behind them was a trail of death and destruction, of crimes and murders of innocent people that we had to stop.

Pedro González was one of the bandits we were determined to get. He committed many murders and was able to create panic in the Trinidad area. One of his last acts was to attack a bus carrying paper workers leaving the factory and traveling along the road from Trinidad to Sancti Spíritus. He set the bus afire and killed some of the workers. Then he ambushed an army vehicle driving by, murdering its occupants.

Pedro González's band would attack somewhere and then he'd immediately split from the rest of the band. He would always go around with only one or two others. That's how he operated. We would capture some members of the band, but González himself always managed to get away.

We pursued him until one Sunday we caught him in what we called an *operación de levante*, a "flush-'em-out operation." We did this when we didn't have enough people for an encirclement. We would take our troops and begin combing the area, until we'd suddenly run into the bandits and they'd have to come into the open and start running. We then knew there were bandits in the area and could estimate how long it would take them to get from here to there. At that point, we could work on putting together an encirclement.

These operations were very important, because we'd manage to keep the bandits on the move, letting us know where they were. Because they were always hiding.

There were times when troops came from Oriente to Las Villas to participate in the operations. In 1963, for example, Compañero Manuel "Tito" Herrera came at the head of a battalion from Oriente. This battalion was armed with FAL light automatic rifles, the most potent gun we had.

Before getting there, the compañeros from Oriente had been told the bandits were just walking around freely in the Escambray. We've gone through forty years of revolution, but back then we were young. We believed if we were sent from Havana to Pinar del Río, then we must be the best, because they were sending us in to resolve the problem. "We're going there to finish it. We'll solve it." Not everyone thought this way, but many did. The compañeros from Oriente arrived thinking that way.

The first days came and our troops didn't see any bandits, since they were hiding. We prepared an operation to comb the area and flush them out. We deployed the Lucha Contra Bandidos battalions from Las Villas, as well as the battalion from Oriente, along the Topes de Collantes highway. That's one of the most mountainous and most difficult areas in the Escambray to comb.

All the compañeros were there. Captain Herrera was at the head of his troops from Oriente. All the people from Las Villas—the Mayaguara Horse and Olaechea—were there too, at the head of their troops. Everyone was marching in single file, mixed in one with another. We combed the area for four days.

What was the result? A number of bandits who had been hiding there heard the noise of the combing operation. Our troops were talking—even though we'd tell them to stop—plus we were using small machetes to clear trails through the undergrowth. Hearing the noise, the bandits fled. They even left their rifles behind.

That operation brought with it an important result—the unity among all the compañeros. There was no more regionalism: "I'm better because I'm from Oriente" or "I'm better because I'm from Las Villas." At moments of danger and struggle, you're not thinking about where you were born; you're thinking that the person beside you is your brother. And you don't care where he's from, only that he's another revolutionary.

Through these actions, our combatants developed a sense of identity. We were LCBers. The members of Lucha Contra Bandidos considered ourselves a single group. You still see it today. The ones who are alive still say, "I'm an LCBer."

Anyway, as we grew stronger, the hour came to eliminate the bandits everywhere.

WATERS: What year was this?

DREKE: In 1964 and 1965. The bandits were eliminated by 1965. I was not in Cuba when they were finally finished off. I had left for the Congo.

But I participated in one of the last operations, as I recall. We captured Mario Bravo, one of the worst bandits, who operated in the Camagüey region, on the border between Sancti Spíritus and Ciego de Avila.

The conditions were being created to take the final step of eliminating the bandits.

State Security had planned an operation to get one of the last groups out of the country and capture them at sea. A ruse was worked out: the bandits thought they were heading to the United States, when they were actually heading straight to jail. The story is told in the movie *The Man of Maisinicú*, a reference to Alberto Delgado. This compañero was a member of State Security who had infiltrated a group of bandits. He lost his life in the line of duty; they murdered him. But the operation was successful.[8]

As the bandits were being eliminated in the Escambray, they were simultaneously being finished off in the rest of the provinces.

At the end a very beautiful rally was held celebrating the elimination of the bandits. I was sorry I wasn't able to be at that celebration, at which our commander in chief spoke.[9]

How were the bandits eliminated? Through the people's unity, the people's determination. Had we not united, we could not have eliminated them, because they kept on and on.

We crushed the bandits. No doubt about it. There are people who don't like saying we crushed them, but we had to crush them. They were assassins and criminals. We never mistreated anyone; the captured bandits were never beaten or abused. But

8. Alberto Delgado, a member of Cuban State Security operating on a farm in Maisinicú in the Escambray, had successfully posed as one of the bandits' key contacts. In March 1964 Delgado arranged to get counterrevolutionary leader Julio Emilio Carretero and his band on a boat supposedly transporting them to the United States. But the "American" boat was actually manned by members of the Cuban armed forces, who apprehended the entire band. José "Cheíto" León, a bandit leader remaining in the Escambray, figured out Delgado's role in the operation and murdered him on April 29, 1964.

The story is described by José Ramón Fernández in *Making History: Interviews with Four Generals of Cuba's Revolutionary Armed Forces* (Pathfinder, 1999), p. 112.

9. On July 26, 1965, the rally marking the twelfth anniversary of the Moncada attack was held in Santa Clara, in Las Villas province. The rally was addressed by Fidel Castro, who spoke of the victory over the bandits. (See introduction, p. 30–31.)

they were taken to serve their sentences, according to what each had done.

It's important to point out the work of many compañeros who pretended to be bandits for a time but who were compañeros from State Security who had infiltrated them. Like Alberto Delgado, "the Man of Maisinicú," and other compañeros who were killed.

Or take the case of Commander Tony Santiago—the same one I fought under during the revolutionary war. He had infiltrated the counterrevolutionary organizations and was an agent for a long time. As far as almost everyone was concerned, he was an enemy who had left Cuba. But he was a compañero from State Security who was carrying out a mission. And they killed him.[10]

Many of these compañeros faced rejection. Not even your father or mother or your wife knew anything. You couldn't even hint at the truth, because your life and the mission were on the line. People didn't know these compañeros were secretly working for State Security. You can imagine how happy these families and others were when they found out the truth.[11]

The job done by the political workers was another important factor in the struggle against the bandits. These compañeros had a big responsibility. Because in addition to combing the woods with a rifle like we had to do, they had the painful and bitter

10. In October 1959, working for Cuban State Security, Santiago pretended to break with the revolution in order to infiltrate the CIA-backed forces. In January 1961 he was killed at sea when his boat was sunk by counterrevolutionary Cuban pirates apparently unaware of his identity. Santiago was heading toward Cuba, where he was to take up a CIA-appointed post as overall head of counterrevolutionary bands in the Escambray.

11. In July 1987 Cuban television began broadcasting a series entitled "The CIA's War against Cuba," which revealed the names of 89 CIA agents in Cuba who had been working as accredited U.S. diplomats. To present this information, Cuba publicly identified 27 Cuban State Security personnel who had been functioning within Cuba as double agents for years. Most of them had had to endure being spurned by family, friends, coworkers, and neighbors. Following the revelations, the 27 were treated as heroes by the Cuban people.

mission of giving a mother the news her son was dead.

One night a compañero was killed who was one of the youngest of our fighters. That day had been his fourteenth birthday. Earlier that day, or the day before, he had been wounded, and he died on his birthday. The family was waiting at home, hoping he'd been given a leave. And the compañeros had to take the body of the young boy to them. It was terrible to see this. Terrible.

There were occasions when compañeros had to bring information to parents and families who were not revolutionaries. That's also true.

Then there was the case of Tartabul. This had a big impact on me personally. As I mentioned earlier, Tartabul had managed to escape the encirclement, the sweep of the area in Manicaragua, against Guillén's band. Tartabul was from Cumanayagua, and his brother was the head of one of our LCB companies.

On the day of the final operation against Tartabul I told his brother, "Look, don't you go," because I knew his brother was there.

"I have to go on the operation," he replied.

"Don't go on the operation. Stay away."

"No, I have to go on the operation." He insisted.

I don't want to give a false picture. He didn't actually come up against his brother face to face. But he wanted to participate in the operation. His mother was a revolutionary, a black woman who didn't understand why her son was with the bandits and not with the rest of the family, who were all revolutionaries.[12]

MADRID: What enabled the bandits to keep functioning? How were they supplied? Who paid them?

DREKE: The bandits were able to function because of the support they received from U.S. imperialism. There's no doubt about that. We don't say it for propaganda purposes, but because it's the truth.

---

12. The bandit Roberto Tartabul was killed in this raid. Three of his brothers were members of Lucha Contra Bandidos.

For one thing, their weapons came from the United States. During the first stage the bandits had a large quantity of weapons—.30 caliber machine guns, and every other type of weapon. We have photos of the weapons they used. These weapons were directly supplied by the Americans. Many were seized, but others remained hidden.

MADRID: Were they sent by air?

DREKE: By air and by sea. A large quantity of weapons came in by sea along the coast extending from Corralillo through Sagua la Chica.

At that time, unbeknown to us, the head of our navy in the Sagua la Grande region, Lt. Ramos, was a traitor. One of his responsibilities was patrolling the coast in that area. And he simply didn't do it, so that weapons could be delivered to the counterrevolutionaries. Ramos eventually took a speedboat and fled Cuba.

Large quantities of weapons were also delivered by air.

The money used by the bandits was sent by the Americans, too. Much of it was sent by way of the counterrevolutionary groups in Cuba that were United States puppets.

They had cadres. They would pull people out of Cuba for training. They had a counterrevolutionary organization inside the country, and a counterrevolutionary organization abroad led by the CIA. Some of these people—such as Evelio Duque, César Páez, Ramonín Quesada, and others—fled during the first cleanup in 1960 and 1961. They were able to escape and leave the country. Others remained in Cuba.

This didn't just happen in the Escambray. The same thing happened in Camagüey. There were clandestine shipments of weapons through Nuevitas. They could do this because during the first years of the revolution, we really didn't have a navy; it consisted of two small boats.

So the aid the bandits got from abroad, from the U.S. government, was essential to their murderous course of conduct and the length of time they were able to survive.

COURTESY PIERO GLEIJESES / CONFLICTING MISSIONS

Shaded areas are those controlled by
rebel forces, August 1964.

Congo

'Africa and Cuba
have influenced
each other deeply.'

Víctor Dreke (left) with Rafael Zerquera (Kumi) and Che Guevara in the Congo, 1965.

The Congo and beyond

From April to November 1965, Víctor Dreke was second in command of a company of 128 Cuban volunteer fighters in the eastern Congo. The column's commander was Ernesto Che Guevara. The internationalist volunteers went to the Congo at the request of liberation forces belonging to the movement founded by Patrice Lumumba. Cuba's goal was to aid them in their fight to defeat the country's pro-imperialist neocolonial regime.

Lumumba was the principal leader of the independence movement in the former Belgian colony and the first prime minister of the Congo. He was the most intransigent of the Congolese leaders, resisting the efforts of the imperialist powers to keep that country under their thumb. A few months after independence was ratified, Lumumba was ousted in a September 1960 coup, organized at the initiative of the U.S. and Belgian rulers. Congolese army chief of staff Joseph Mobutu was the willing tool of these powers. Lumumba, who had been placed under the "protection" of United Nations troops, was captured and then murdered in January 1961 by forces loyal to Moise Tshombe. Tshombe was leading an imperialist-backed secessionist movement in the Congolese province of Katanga.

In mid-1964 forces that had been part of Lumumba's movement launched a new revolt against the neocolonial regime. The rebels were able to gain control of Stanleyville (today Kisangani), the country's second-largest city. In November 1964, however, they were defeated with the help of Belgian and white South African mercenary forces—politically and militarily backed by Washington—whose mission was to prevent the Congo's vast mineral wealth from escaping imperialist control. Thousands were massacred as the mercenary forces retook Stanleyville.

Despite the defeat, large numbers of rebel fighters regrouped in several areas of the country. These were the forces that turned to Cuba and others for help. In response, Cuban volunteers came to the Congo to assist in their training and to support their struggle. In carrying out this internationalist mission, the leadership of the Cuban contingent worked together with other anti-imperialist forces in Africa, especially the revolutionary government of Ahmed Ben Bella in Algeria. The international effort to support the Congolese rebel forces also had the official backing of the Organization of African Unity (OAU).

In June 1965, as the Cuban volunteer contingent in the Congo was still getting established in Algeria, the government of Ahmed Ben Bella was overturned by defense minister Houari Boumedienne. The military coup was a major blow to revolutionary anti-imperialist forces in Africa and undermined continued support to the struggle in the Congo. In October 1965 the OAU withdrew support for the fight against the proimperialist regime. Owing to the OAU decision, as well as deep divisions and other weaknesses in the leadership of the forces in the Congo, the Cuban volunteers, at the request of the Congolese, withdrew in November 1965.

Most of the internationalist volunteers rapidly returned to Cuba. Guevara and several others went to Tanzania, however, where they remained for several months while preparations were made to open a revolutionary front in Bolivia. While there, Guevara wrote *Episodes of the Revolutionary War: Congo,* using the campaign diary he had kept as a reference. The manuscript of the *Episodes,* as prepared and edited by Guevara, was first published 33 years later, in April 1999.

Despite its outcome, Che's Congo mission was irreplaceable preparation for Cuban support to other liberation movements throughout sub-Saharan Africa, including Angola, Mozambique, Ethiopia, and Guinea-Bissau.

In Cuba's largest internationalist mission ever, between 1975 and 1989, more than 300,000 combatants served in Angola, helping to defend that country against a South African invasion and an imperialist-backed insurgency, once again supported by Washington. In

Nelson Mandela's words, Cuba's support was "a milestone in the history of the struggle for southern African liberation" and "a turning point in the struggle to free the continent and our country from the scourge of apartheid."

■

WATERS: With the publication of Che's *Episodes of the Revolutionary War: Congo* a few months ago, it has become possible, for the first time, for those of us outside Cuba to begin to have accurate information about this chapter of our revolutionary history.[1]

You were second in command of the Cuban forces in the Congo, working directly under Che's orders, and are in a unique position to talk about this mission.

How did it begin? What led to the decision to send volunteers to the Congo?

DREKE: In the 1960s not only was there a very intense struggle within Cuba to defend the revolution against U.S. imperialism's efforts to destroy us. Struggles against U.S. imperialism were advancing outside Cuba too. Around the world national liberation movements were intensifying their struggles to free their people from colonialism and imperialist domination. This was especially true in Africa.

The struggle in the Congo led by Patrice Lumumba first attempted to achieve independence from Belgian colonial rule by peaceful means. This failed. The imperialists said yes to independence, but it was all a lie.

As that reality became clear, Lumumba decided the only possibility of achieving the liberation of the Congo was through armed struggle. But in January 1961 they murdered him. The

---

1. The Spanish edition was published by Grijalbo-Mondadori. An English-language edition was published by The Harvill Press (London) in 2000 and by Grove Press (New York) in 2001, under the title *The African Dream: The Diaries of the Revolutionary War in the Congo.*

assassination of Patrice Lumumba had great repercussions around the world. We felt them here in Cuba.

As you know, Fidel's position, the revolution's position, was to support liberation movements, to support the liberation and independence of all peoples on whatever continent. Even though we were deeply immersed in the struggle in the Americas, we were not strangers to the situation in Africa, nor that of other peoples.

In late 1964 and early 1965 Commander Guevara made a tour through Africa. While there, he went to many countries and met many African leaders. He got a concrete feel for the situation in Africa. He saw there was an upsurge of revolutionary struggle, and that the Congolese were fighting to avenge the murder of Patrice Lumumba and to take power from the neocolonial government installed by the imperialist powers.

Meanwhile here in Cuba we were responding to a request from the leaders of Lumumba's movement, among them Laurent Kabila. They had requested that we assist them by sending instructors to the Congo. First, actually, they asked to send a group of Congolese compañeros to train in Cuba. The response by Commander Guevara, which can be found in his book about the revolutionary war in the Congo—and this was Fidel's response as well—was that it's better to do the training on the ground, in the Congo. The Congolese accepted this, and they also accepted the offer of having Cuban instructors on the ground, who would at the same time fight as part of the liberation struggle.

This was not interference on our part. The Congolese requested Cuba's involvement. Besides, at that time the Belgians, the Americans, the French, everybody was in there. Imperialism was giving assistance to counterrevolutionary forces everywhere. And imperialism in those years was launching deadly attacks aimed at destroying the Cuban Revolution—just as today, except now they put a different face on their attacks. Therefore, the Cuban Revolution had both the right and the duty to defend itself with all weapons and all means at our disposal. It's important to understand this historical context and to place ourselves in the situation that existed then.

In order to help the Congolese liberate themselves, we decided to provide them the assistance they asked for. One day in early 1965, while Che was continuing on his tour in Africa, I was summoned to the Central Army headquarters. This was in the midst of the operation against one of the last bandits. I was told I should report immediately to the Central Army General Staff headquarters to see the Central Army's commander, Calixto García.

I reported there, and the head of the army asked me if I was willing to fulfill a mission, an internationalist mission. Of course I said yes.

"When do I leave?"

"Not yet."

I was given orders to select a group of compañeros for the mission from the Central Army, in this case from the Lucha Contra Bandidos. So I went about the task of selecting a group of twenty to thirty compañeros—a company. They were to be from among the most courageous compañeros, with combat experience. At that time our combat experience came from the compañeros of the Rebel Army, the struggle against the bandits, and Girón. Those were the yardsticks we had to measure a compañero's experience. Furthermore, I was told, the compañeros were to be black—"very black." That was the instruction I was given.

I began to select the compañeros very discreetly.

I'd take them aside and ask: "Are you willing to . . . ?" I'd tell the compañero I didn't know how long it would be: "Five years at least." He'd say yes.

What happened then?

The compañero would immediately leave with us. The jeep was outside. The compañero would grab his pack and get in the jeep. Then we'd go to another company and do the same thing. After visiting three companies we had four black men in the jeep. Nobody said anything to anyone, only that he was going away.

Other people would see us and say, "Hey, I want to go too. Take me along."

"No, we're not going anywhere. We're just on our way to an operation."

"An operation with five men? Where the hell are these guys going?"

The same thing was simultaneously being done, in the same way, in the Eastern Army, by Capt. Santiago Terry. In the Western Army it was done by Lt. Normando Agramonte, who currently is our ambassador to Congo-Brazzaville.

In this way we formed a company, which was the term used for this group. Although at other times we referred to it as a column.

The men were brought separately to Havana. Some came from one area, some from another. We went to the Pedro Marrero stadium, where we met with Manuel Piñeiro, Captain Luis Pérez, who was head of Unit 1546—which is where the compañeros in Pinar del Río were trained—First Lieutenant Luis Matos, head of medical services, and Ulises Estrada of the Ministry of the Interior.

Piñeiro had already told me I'd been designated head of the mission, that I had to train those men. The rest of the compañeros arrived, and on February 2, 1965, the company was formed—a company that was to fulfill a mission none of us knew where.

Of course, there were so many compañeros who were black that everyone thought it would be Africa. We didn't know if it would be the Congo or somewhere else. But people began to whisper. Earlier the men had been told they shouldn't even talk to each other about the mission, so people were being careful. But almost everybody had an idea about it.

A company of riflemen was established; two or three compañeros were added for artillery. Combat training for this column began in February. The first group left in April. Another group stayed behind in training.

The compañeros from the Congo had requested a contingent of thirty. A decision was made to send up to a company, up to a column, in order to provide the support needed to defend ourselves. You can't defend yourself with thirty men. In addition, Che had proposed that these compañeros—that is, us—participate in armed actions.

None of us, including myself, had any idea Che was going to be on this mission. Che never visited the camp; he never came by. He was abroad on a tour; we listened to news about it on the radio.

We continued our combat training. The commander in chief came a number of times. Fidel participated in target practice, gave instructions, issued passes to the compañeros sometimes so they could go home, since we had picked them up directly from the camps where they were stationed and brought them there. We were to tell our families we were going to the Soviet Union. Imagine, so many blacks going to the Soviet Union!

MADRID: All of you said you were on your way to the Soviet Union?

DREKE: That's all the volunteers were to say: "To the Soviet Union for five years, I'll write you later. I'll write you once I know the address. Right now you can't write me. We don't know where we're going to be staying. We're going to take a language course." Most of the compañeros had not even completed fifth or sixth grade. Yet we were supposed to be taking language courses. That's what families were told.

I want to emphasize that keeping it a secret from our families was very important. Because you can imagine what would have happened if the imperialists had found out. We wouldn't have gotten there; they would have prevented it.

This was one of the blows that hurt imperialism the most, I believe. It's one of the many blows the commander has dealt them. Each time they fire at us, Fidel has an answer. But they knew nothing about this. Much less that Che was going. They were left twisting in the wind.

So we continued our training. On March 30 compañero Osmany Cienfuegos appeared. He told me the commander in chief had decided I was not going to head up the column.

I said fine, but I insisted on my right to participate, even if I didn't head up the column.

Yes, he told me, you're going to go. Furthermore, he said, the compañero who will head up the column is a good person. "He's a very good friend of yours. You know each other very well. You won't have any problems."

"I don't have problems with anyone," I said.

Osmany showed me some photographs.

"This is compañero Ramón, and he has been designated head of the column. He holds the rank of commander." That's all Osmany told me, that he was a commander.

I took a look at the photo and didn't recognize this commander. I was also a commander at the time. There weren't many with that rank, and we all knew each other. We had fought together in the war, or else we had been together at some time at some meeting. "Where did this commander come from?" I asked myself.

"I don't know him," I said.

"Christ, pal, how can you not recognize him?" Osmany said. "You know him well. I know you know him."

"No, I don't know who he is," I repeated. "Okay, commander," I told Osmany. "We'll see."

The next day, March 31, Osmany picked me up and took me to a house somewhere. When I arrived "Papi" was there—José María Martínez Tamayo. Papi and I didn't know each other, so Osmany introduced us.

Osmany had already explained Papi's history to me on the way to the house. He told me how brave Papi was, how unafraid to take risks. But he didn't tell me Papi worked closely with Che; he never mentioned Che.

So there I was in the house. When I came in, I noticed a man with his back to us who was writing at a table. Osmany went up to him and said something. Almost immediately the gentleman stood up and came over.

"This is the compañero who is going to head up the column, to whom you'll be subordinate," Osmany said, introducing us.

I didn't recognize him. I didn't know him. It wasn't just a

matter of looking at a photograph and not recognizing him. He was standing right in front of me, close up, and I still didn't recognize him.

Then Che spoke and told me who he was. That was one of the most unforgettable moments of my life, when he said he was Che. Even then, I still didn't recognize him. Anyway, we stayed there for a while, and then he went back to his writing.

I wanted to explain to him the whole history of the column, how it had been formed and all that. But he already knew it all. He asked me about specifics, about certain compañeros who had had small problems. He asked about those particular individuals. So I understood right away that Che was well informed about everything that had happened.

Later that day, the commander in chief came and spoke with Che, Osmany, Papi, and me. There's a photo of this. Fidel explained the mission and gave us encouragement. He told us we'd have all the support we needed. That our families would be fine; that we shouldn't worry about them.

At one point I noticed that Che gave an envelope to Fidel. I later concluded it must have been Che's farewell letter.[2]

On the morning of April 1 the three of us left Cuba—Che, Papi, and me. We left from Havana. Osmany took us to the airport. We were carrying diplomatic passports . . . and "diplomatic" pistols.

We arrived in Tanzania by a long circuitous route. When we got there something very similar happened with compañero Pablo Rivalta, who was our ambassador in Tanzania.

Rivalta had been in Che's unit during the war of liberation and was a good friend. And we introduced him to Che the same way Che had been introduced to me. We weren't trying to pull Rivalta's leg but—just as Osmany had done with me—to verify that Che really couldn't be recognized.

---

2. Guevara's farewell letter to Fidel Castro is contained in *The Bolivian Diary of Ernesto Che Guevara* (Pathfinder, 1994), pp. 71–73 and *Episodes of the Cuban Revolutionary War (1956–58)*, pp. 420–22.

There's a photo taken as the commander was saying goodbye to us, where Fidel is checking out Che's passport. This was important. We had to go through several different countries. So I imagine this test was performed on a number of people in addition to ourselves, to make sure Che couldn't be recognized.

Anyway, we introduced Che as a compañero who was part of our group and asked Rivalta if he knew him. Rivalta already knew we were headed for the Congo. He had been in touch with Rogelio Oliva, who was to be our direct contact with the Cuban embassy in Tanzania, and with the Congolese. Rogelio was the only one of us who knew Swahili.

"No, I don't know him," Rivalta said. He was staring at Che, with an odd look on his face.

"So, Pablo, you're still the same shit-eater you always were!" said Che, on one of those impulses he was famous for.

Pablo Rivalta began to wheeze and sob right there in the airport.

"Cut it out, damn it," we said, "cut it out! Look at you, a big guy blubbering so!"

We always used to talk like that to each other. I should explain that, because when you publish this story, some people are going to say, "That's what we always said about Che, that he abused people." No, the truth is that they knew each other very well and Che was very fond of Pablo.

Pablo had been part of Che's column that had carried out the invasion from Oriente to Las Villas. The story is that along the route Pablo was carrying a number of documents and books that Che had been reading. There was an ambush; the army surprised them. They had to get out of there in a hurry, and Pablo lost some of Che's books. I can imagine the chewing-out Che gave him. So Che was repeating what he had said to Pablo back then.

What's more, when Che spoke he did so in his own voice. And hearing Che's voice, Pablo couldn't contain his shock.

Anyway, in Tanzania we had our first meeting with the leadership in the Congo. Kabila wasn't present. We met with Godefroid Tchamlesso and some others. We explained to them what our idea was in coming to the Congo. The commander in chief had given us strict orders that we were completely under their command, we said. And we explained that instead of the thirty compañeros they had requested, there would be about a hundred of us. We explained the whole story.

We told them Che was our doctor and translator, and that Papi was a compañero who also had guerrilla experience and was coming as the doctor's assistant. We had to give some explanation, since Che and Papi were white and, as I said earlier, all the participants were supposed to be black, "very black."

The plan was that we would leave right away for the Congo. But things weren't ready. There were some weapons; that part had been prepared the best. But we needed boots, blankets, and various other provisions. And the compañeros responsible to make sure everything was ready were just beginning to organize it. They went off to get the things that were needed.

The Congolese agreed that, yes, there could be a hundred men; that wasn't a problem.

It was about a week before the first group of fourteen could leave. In Che's account you can find the names of all those who made up that first group. Che took advantage of those days to explain his thinking to us. He also gave each of us a Swahili name. He took for himself the name "Tatu," which means Three. Papi was "Mbili" (Two), and I was "Moja" (One). We took the first three numbers, and Che went on naming them in order as they joined us, two or three at a time, up to the fourteenth.

By the time we were up to ten compañeros, Che was anxious to get going. But transportation across the lake wasn't ready. Che was worried that one of our groups coming in would be detected, making it impossible to get into the Congo. And he was concerned that as a result of an indiscretion or something, people would find out that Che himself was there. His concern wasn't his own physical safety. As a revolutionary, he was worried about not being able to carry out the mission.

There were two risks. One was that the enemy would discover

Che's identity. The other was that the Congolese would learn who he was, and wouldn't agree to Che entering the combat zone. That's why Che was in such a hurry to leave.

"Let's get going, the ten of us."

Finally the last eight compañeros arrived. Fourteen of us went into the Congo and four stayed behind, either because they were sick or for lack of equipment.

"They'll be all right in two days," said Kumi [Rafael Zerquera], who was there as the doctor. "We can wait two days."

"No, two days is out of the question," Che said. "Let them wait and come with the next group."

And that's what we did.

Tchamlesso, the Congolese compañero we called "Tremendo Punto" went along with us.

We got to Kigoma, which is where you board the boat. Because of problems with the boat, however, we couldn't leave on the night of April 22, which is when we were supposed to. So we left the next night, the 23rd, and we got there early on the morning of the 24th. We disembarked at Kibamba.

It was a difficult journey; the boat took on water along the way. In addition, the Congolese were singing and dancing, as was their custom. They were in danger, but they sang and danced and played musical instruments.

"Be quiet," we'd say. But they wouldn't be quiet. That's how things were. We didn't understand that.

We were in the middle of the lake, carrying out a dangerous landing operation, and the Congolese said, "Look at the lights." They told us those were the lights of Tshombe's patrol boats. There we were in the middle of the lake, where you can't shout, you can't talk. Voices carry a long way. But they didn't pay any attention to us. They kept on singing and playing, until we finally arrived on the opposite bank without anyone noticing us.

That was our first contact with the Congolese guerrillas.

Che gave orders to scout the area to see where we were. We decided to stay in that camp for a couple of days, and then go to another base higher up, on the highest hill in the area. We went

Shaded areas are those controlled by
rebel forces, early 1965.

Eastern Congo, 1965

to scout out the place to prepare the conditions to go up there.

One day Che decided to reveal who he was to Tremendo Punto, and through him send a message to Kabila. Because Kabila didn't know either. Kabila knew some Cubans had arrived, but he didn't know who. Just that a certain Moja, an officer in the Cuban army, had come in with a group of Cubans.

So Che had a meeting with Tremendo Punto and explained that he was Che. It was a great shock. Tremendo Punto began to shout, "Scandal! International scandal!" He put his hands on his head and started to run, as if someone were chasing him. "International scandal!" That's what he insisted it would be when it was learned that Che was there under arms, as part of that guerrilla army.

So Che gave him a message to send to Kabila, saying that Che was there and that he was placing himself completely under Kabila's orders.

In the next few days Che got sick. He came down with malaria, complicated by his asthma. He had a very high fever. We discussed his condition, and our doctor dared suggest to Che, very delicately, that he be sent to Cuba, that he be gotten out of there to recuperate. Che nearly killed him.

"I'm not leaving this place," Che said.

But the truth was he had a bad case. And we were all frightened.

We had heard people talk about malaria, but we didn't know what it was. Then Che got sick, with pain in his limbs, vomiting, with a fever of 40 degrees [104° F]. He was delirious, saying all kinds of things. Moreover, we were there on that mountain, where it was so cold everyone's teeth were chattering. Later on, when others of us got sick with malaria, it no longer frightened us. That day it did.

WATERS: In his introduction to *Episodes of the Revolutionary War: Congo* Che remarks, "This is the history of a decomposition of our own fighting morale." It's important to understand what happened and why, he says, in order to draw the lessons for other fighters in the future. The enemies of the revolution campaign around this question, saying it was a colossal defeat, a total adventure. We're interested in what you think. What's your balance sheet?

DREKE: My opinions are based on the time I spent with Che. I got to know him a little. There are compañeros who spent more years with him. But I had the opportunity to be with him at that particular time and to know what he thought about Africa.

So helping to tell this story is a responsibility I have, a historic duty. The revolution gave me this privilege. The commander in chief and the minister [Fidel Castro and Raúl Castro] gave me the privilege of participating in this action with Che. It could have been done by some other compañero. There were thousands of compañeros ready and willing to leave Cuba with Che, compañeros equally qualified, or more qualified than I—thousands of them. But it fell to me. That means I have a historic responsibility to fulfill.

First of all, I can tell you that every word Che wrote in the book, absolutely every letter, without changing so much as a comma, happened the way Che said. There's no question about it.

When people refer to what happened in the Congo as a failure, they're simply using Che's own words. They take the difficult moments Che was going through when he made this assessment—and Che always wrote exactly what he was thinking, what he was living through at any particular time. Enemies of the revolution seize this for their own purposes. The faint-hearts seize it too, and perhaps some confused individuals.

When Che raised leaving Cuba, and told us it would take five years, at a minimum, in order to accomplish anything, I don't think he was thinking of taking the whole Congo. The Congo isn't Guanabacoa.[3]

Che said five years. If it turned out we had had the five years, and we weren't able to win the victory Che was thinking of, then for him that would have been a defeat. Che didn't use half-way terms to refer to himself. For Che it was black or white. It wasn't

3. Guanabacoa is a small town just east of Havana.

half-black or half-white. It was black or white. You either win or you lose. I think that was one of Che's expressions: "We have to win, we can't lose."

In his book, Che's assessment is that the operation was a failure. But he left the door open so that later others could give their opinion, and it could be analyzed with the passage of time and events.

Thirty-four years have passed. Every time someone interviews me about this, I try to find a way, first of all, to always tell the truth. Second, not to create confusion. And third, not to cause divisions. Because we think that everything that divides us at this time is bad. We have to unite.

But I think Che would make a different assessment if he were doing it now. I'm absolutely sure of that. He would continue to say we should've won, that we were fighting to win and didn't. But there are things you'll see in the book that Che blames himself for, and when you analyze the situation you'll see they weren't Che's fault at all.

There were problems he couldn't resolve. First, because 128 men can't change the characteristics of an African country like the Congo. Che did everything he could. If it weren't for Che, instead of the war lasting seven months from the time we arrived, it would have been all over in two months. Because when we arrived in the Congo, there was practically no war; it hardly existed.

We thought that everything there was ready, that there were armies in the field. That all they needed was some military training.

We didn't have an accurate picture. We didn't have totally correct information on the situation in the Congo. Much of the information we'd gotten through various sources had been obtained in the capitals of different countries. And unfortunately, in many liberation movements—not just in the Congo but in other places too—the compañeros have a habit of exaggerating. If they capture a rifle they say they captured ten rifles. If they kill a soldier they say it was twenty soldiers. This wasn't true of the Cuban Revolution. In reporting on events we never claimed a single extra bullet, a single extra enemy killed, a single extra prisoner. And at the time, we thought the Congolese were the same as us. I have to say this in all honesty. We assumed they thought like us. We thought some Congolese leader was Fidel Castro, Raúl Castro, Almeida, Ameijeiras, and so on.

But it was different. One thing that shocked us was that the main leaders of the Congo liberation movement were not there on the front lines. But when you look more deeply at the liberation struggle in Africa, you see that the same thing was happening all over.

All the African liberation movements were based in neighboring countries. They developed on the border, in neighboring countries. We didn't understand this. We were young people accustomed to Fidel being with us day and night, side by side, or Almeida, who was in charge of operations in the Escambray. The compañeros were right there on the front lines of battle. But in Africa it was different.

As you will read in Che's account, the Congolese relied on *dawa*. This was witchcraft, a religious ritual they practiced. They relied on it to fight, to move. "If you take two or three hours doing that, the soldiers are going to capture us," we'd say to them. But they relied on it.

We had other misconceptions too. Speaking truthfully, almost nobody here knew anything about Africa. Our image was from Tarzan movies—Tarzan and Cheeta the monkey. That was all we knew about Africa. And when we read the little bit that was available about the history of Africa in those days, we still didn't know anything. Because the history we were reading at the institute or in schools of higher education was written by the capitalists, by the colonial exploiters of Africa. It didn't tell the truth about Africa. So almost nobody here knew anything at all about Africa, leaving aside some leaders who did have some knowledge.

Even today, thirty-four years later, what we know is limited. Even the Africans themselves don't know everything about Africa. There are places on the continent even they don't know about. And thirty-four years ago it was worse, since there were few means of communication, no news, no radio, no nothing.

We might be together with five African compañeros, and each would be speaking a different dialect. Che spoke French, but most of them didn't understand French. Only the leaders understood French, and to talk to the leaders you had to go to Kigoma in Tanzania, or to France. Ordinary people didn't speak French. It was necessary to learn Swahili.

Che chastised himself for not having learned Swahili. But how many more things was the commander going to learn? He was our teacher, he gave classes in mathematics, he gave classes in Spanish, he gave classes in philosophy, he gave a group of us classes in *Capital,* he was a doctor, he was a guerrilla. And is he supposed to be a teacher of Swahili on top of all that? It was something Che blamed himself for, a lack of Swahili. I imagine that if he had known all this before he left, he would have studied Swahili in Cuba. We should've learned it. But we didn't know that beforehand. That's the fact.

What were some of the other factors?

In terms of the Cubans, there were some compañeros who asked to go home, who decided to leave—very few, when you count them up. We don't consider these compañeros in their majority to be cowards. It wasn't a question of cowardice; they simply didn't understand.

These were young men who were eighteen or nineteen years old at the time, some twenty to twenty-five. Young men who, to all intents and purposes, had grown up under the revolution. They were thinking of our guerrilla struggle, which had been different. A number of them had only completed third or fourth grade. It wasn't that we recruited illiterates. It's just that before the revolution triumphed a large portion of the population of Cuba had been illiterate or semiliterate, especially in the rural areas. Moreover, it was the least educated who were generally the most courageous, the best revolutionary soldiers, because they were defending the working class. Even though there were some students with a high educational level who were very revo-

lutionary, the great majority of those who were making the revolution at that time—which was only four or five years after the
victory—were proletarians. The poorest people, the most
humble.

What's more, when from within this poorest and most humble
layer, you selected only blacks, the educational level dropped
even lower. That's the truth about the history of our country.
Before the revolution, the illiteracy rate was higher among
blacks. And at that time, in 1965, blacks still had a lower educational level. Remember that this was occurring just six years after
the triumph of the revolution and four years after the literacy
campaign. And this reality was reflected in the fact that some
of these compañeros didn't understand.

They didn't understand something fundamental: As a revolutionary, Che felt he was the equal of any of us, in a personal
sense, but that he had to give more, he had to do more than the
rest of us. That's the way he was. These compañeros didn't understand why Che was there risking his life while the Congolese leaders weren't even there. These troops didn't understand
this. That's the historical truth.

And what was the reaction? Some said, "I want to leave."
Some said, "I'll die somewhere else, but I'm not going to die here
because these people don't fight."

Some of the Cuban compañeros in the Congo who said they
wanted to go home later went on to participate in the liberation
struggle in Guinea-Bissau. They fought in Angola and Ethiopia,
they were in Nicaragua and other countries. And some of them
died in those countries. In other words, it wasn't a question of
fear or cowardice.

We have to say in all honesty, and in tribute to Che, that he
was clear about what was happening, and this is reflected in his
book. Even though he fought firmly against some of the prevail-
ing attitudes.

These were very difficult moments for Che. For one thing, as
he explains in the book, he wanted to be at the front with his
troops. But he was at the camp, with Pombo—about a two- or

three- or four-day march from the rest of the troops operating in the field.

MADRID: Why couldn't Che be there at the front with you?

DREKE: One reason was that the main leader, compañero Kabila, the current president of the Congo, had told Che to wait for him. "Wait for me there and I'll come." And Soumialot too, "Wait for me there and I'll come." So Che couldn't just leave without seeing Kabila and go to the front.

Finally—as he explains in his book—he "escaped" and came to join us. Che broke the rules. He left with two or three men. He sent me a note one day saying, "Listen, any day now I'm going to escape."

He took a great risk by just leaving. If I had known about it ahead of time, I would've sent some soldiers to accompany him. But that's the way Che was. If he hadn't done that, he wouldn't have been Che.

WATERS: When you went to Africa, were you thinking of more than just the Congo?

DREKE: Che went with the idea of being able to unite all the Africans. His approach, as you'll see in the book, was not just to train this group but also to establish a camp where later fighters from other countries in Africa could be trained. At a certain point he recognized it wasn't possible at that time to bring Africans from different countries together in unity in the Congo. But Che couldn't simply accept that.

There is the concrete case of the Rwandans who were part of our forces. The Congolese wouldn't accept them. But Che, with his idea of how things should develop, his idea of unity, rejected this; he thought unity was possible. So did I. After all, I thought, we had achieved unity in Cuba. At one point, I thought it would be just like the Escambray, where we'd united all the revolutionary forces under Che's orders. That's what I thought, I can't deny it. But afterwards, as time went on, I came to realize it wasn't to be.

Everything was different over there. We wanted to change certain things. Their superiors used to beat soldiers, for example.

Che was against this, as all of us were. We finally managed to stop soldiers from being beaten inside the Cuban camp. That was our first accomplishment. We got there one day and someone was being beaten; it looked like they were going to beat the poor guy to death, and he was screaming about I don't know what. Someone said he was a counterrevolutionary, or a spy. But there was no State Security, no investigation of spies. We stopped the beating.

There were many personal problems, problems of tribalism, various squabbles. The families lived in the camps, the women, the children. Children had also participated in our war, but as combatants. Children were part of the peasant rear guard in Cuba. Some children were real combatants, with rifles on their shoulders. They had to fight if the army came. But the families of our fighters didn't live in the camps. In the Congo this was a tradition we couldn't break. Che was unable to change it.

People loved Che because he was a doctor—"Doctor Tatu" they called him. They saw him more as a doctor than a guerrilla. Because he went to the people. You sometimes see photographs of children there being carried by Che. He wasn't carrying them to pose for a photo. That's just the way Che was.

Even though he seemed very harsh to some, Che had feelings, he was affectionate. He loved his men, he respected his men, he watched over his men, and he was concerned about everyone. When he told you, "Do this," it was because he too was capable of doing it.

Che used to give us words of encouragement, especially at the most difficult moments.

"Fidel kept the struggle going with fewer men," he would say. "Fidel was left with twelve men, and we went on to victory.[4] The

4. On December 5, 1956, three days after landing in southeastern Cuba, the *Granma* expeditionaries were surprised by the Batista army. Of the eighty-two combatants, half were murdered or imprisoned. In the third week of December, twelve of the expeditionaries had reassembled in the Sierra Maestra mountains. In the following months a quarter of the expedition members were able to regroup, forming the core of the Rebel Army.

only thing to regret here is that Fidel isn't with us, that Fidel Castro is not the one in charge here."

This was an expression of the affection, the respect, the admiration Che had for Fidel—contrary to the attempts of some to portray divisions between Che and Fidel.

This was also Che's attitude toward Raúl Castro. Che's respect, his affection for Raúl, his admiration for Raúl was very great.

Some people have tried to spread slanders around this. They've used the traitor Benigno, for example, to try to slander Che and insinuate shady things about him, talking about conflicts between Che, Fidel, and Raúl. Not to mention the lies he tells us about the Congo.

Despite what he says, Benigno was never in the Congo.[5] He never set foot in the Congo. He says I gave him a strange name. I don't even remember the name he says I gave him. But I never gave anybody a name in the Congo. I was the second-in-command of the troops in the Congo.

Here in Cuba, before Che arrived, I was in command of Che's troops. That was here in Cuba, and only until Che took charge himself. Here in Cuba, the names we assigned were Cuban names. Not African names. And Benigno wasn't even in the camp with us in Cuba.

The same thing with [Jonas] Savimbi. Savimbi was never with Che's troops. That's just a lie, a complete falsehood.

WATERS: Why was there such a great difference between the information you had about the situation in the Congo before you left and the reality you encountered when you got there? Good intelligence work has generally been one of the strengths of the Cuban Revolution.

DREKE: Yes, over the years the Cuban Revolution has kept improving its intelligence services. But our intelligence work at

---

5. "Benigno" was a nom-de-guerre of Dariel Alarcón, a former Cuban combatant who had fought with Che in Bolivia in 1966 and was one of three Cuban survivors. In 1996 he left Cuba, and began to peddle false stories about the Cuban Revolution and its leaders, with the aim of creating divisions.

that time was not directed toward Africa.

I think today nobody could surprise us about Africa. But at that time we *were* surprised. The compañeros who went to make a study of the conditions in Africa went there to the lake. They went to Kigoma. They saw the Congolese troops and talked to them. And the Congolese troops told them all kinds of tall tales.

If I had gone, I might have done the same thing. Maybe not, because I was a guerrilla. I might have said, "Take me to see the front line. I'm going to stick around for a week in order to go with you, to take part in combat." Perhaps the Congolese compañeros would not have let us go observe a guerrilla unit, or participate in an action. I don't know.

In any case, the information we had here in Cuba was what the Africans had told us. But when we got there, it wasn't how they described it.

MADRID: Was this also true of the Congolese leaders who came to Cuba?

DREKE: Along these lines, I'll say something here about Soumialot's visit to Cuba. This occurred while we were in the Congo.

Everything Soumialot told compañeros here in Cuba was a lie. Because he had never come to see us, he had never seen Che. Yet here he was in Cuba telling stories. He extracted a promise of fifty Cuban doctors, as if you could put fifty doctors there. Fortunately, compañero Machado, who was the minister of health, went to see Che in the Congo, and Che explained things to him, and took him different places. Machadito realized there was no place to put fifty doctors, that only the six or seven or eight doctors we had there made sense, because there was no place for them. Just imagine: What if Machadito hadn't gone there and we had sent fifty doctors?

And how would fifty doctors have gotten there? It wasn't easy to get to the Congo. We had managed to break through the cordon. That's why the Americans were angry, as I told you, because our compañeros got there through various capitalist countries around the world. They did so all with the same kind of suitcase, outfit, and suit of clothes. Just imagine four blacks wearing identical hats in the airport in Italy. The poor guys had never been out of Santiago de Cuba. They couldn't speak the language, didn't know anybody. You would see them in France, in Cairo, in Italy, all over. Yet they all managed to get to the Congo, I don't know how.

MADRID: They were all dressed alike?

DREKE: All dressed alike, with the same type suitcase and everything.

What helped was that nobody said a word, everybody was disciplined. Nobody let anything out of the bag. Of course, none of them knew Che was there. But they were very disciplined.

It's worth stating that today, after thirty-four years, out of that column of 128 men, only one—who married a foreigner—has left the country, and he's never spoken ill of Cuba. This fact is a demonstration of loyalty. This is important, although no one has written about it. Where are the members of Che's column in the Congo? The ones still alive are right here in Cuba today.

WATERS: What were the circumstances in which the Cuban volunteers left the Congo?

DREKE: At a certain point we realized the thing was lost, that the Congolese themselves had made a decision to end the fighting. We decided to keep fifteen combatants there.

We suggested to Che that he leave.

"*I'm* staying because I'm the one in charge here," he answered angrily.

What was involved? If we had left the Congo without an official request from them to do so, then thirty-four years later someone could say that Che had run away from the Congo. But no one can say that. Did the Cubans run away from the Congo? No, we left at their request and with their authorization, and after repeated urgings by African leaders from other countries, not just the Congolese.

Even when we were withdrawing from the Congo, when everybody was getting out, Che never gave in.

"You have to maintain discipline, Moja. Discipline has to be maintained. If we don't, this will turn into a free-for-all." Those were his words.

Because there were times when we went into battle and the Congolese compañeros who were fighting alongside us just ran away and abandoned their weapons.

"Cubans have to retreat with elegance," Che insisted. "We can't run helter-skelter."

"Retreating with elegance" meant you ran two steps, fired two shots, ran some more, fired two more shots. We couldn't leave in a stampede, throwing away our weapons, throwing away our shoes, throwing everything away. That was Che's opinion.

We left armed; we crossed the lake arms in hand. We installed a 75 mm cannon on one of the boats. It was a suicidal thing to do, because if we had fired that cannon in the middle of the lake, the boat would've sunk. It was one of those little boats. But that was our idea of how we would leave the Congo.

We knew we couldn't win the war, but we weren't handing over our weapons. We weren't surrendering, with our hands above our heads. We weren't asking anybody's pardon. We didn't ask for priests or ministers or anybody else to come rescue us. We left with our weapons in our hands. That's something history cannot forget.

I think that today, thirty-four years later, we see the positive result of that action. The action of those compañeros who fell in the Congo was not in vain. As Raúl Castro said in 1985, the Congo operation was multiplied in other actions in Africa.[6] The experience we gained made it possible for us to do what we did to aid the liberation struggles in Guinea-Bissau, Angola, and other places.

WATERS: You said earlier that "Today nobody could surprise us about Africa." You yourself, three and a half decades later, continue to be deeply involved in the political work of the Cu-

---

6. This speech is printed in Jorge Risquet Valdés, *El segundo frente del Che en el Congo: Historia del Batallón Patricio Lumumba* (Havana: Casa Editora Abril, 2000), pp. 10–15.

ban Revolution in relation to Africa. How have you maintained those ties?

DREKE: Ever since the internationalist mission to the Congo I've had strong ties to Africa.

I didn't consider the mission a defeat, although we hadn't achieved what we'd been asked to do, what we wanted to do, or what was necessary. And we thought we could accomplish other things.

Upon our return from Africa, we were greeted by the commander in chief and the minister of the armed forces. They listened to our opinions with great interest and attention. Both of them encouraged us to continue the fight. And they met with the members of the column.

At first our idea was to keep the column intact so we'd be able to carry out other missions. Later we changed our view on that, and each compañero was reintegrated into the Western, Central, or Eastern Army, wherever they had previously come from, or else they went to school.

I continued in the Revolutionary Armed Forces, and I also maintained my links with Africa. When we left the Congo, a number of Africans returned to Cuba with us, and one of them came to live in my home. He was like a member of my family. His name was Sumba and here we called him Fidelito. He was killed after returning to the Congo to fight.

Soon after that, in 1966, I left for my first mission to Guinea-Bissau. I headed up our military mission there and in the Republic of Guinea. Keep in mind that Guinea-Bissau was still under Portuguese colonial rule, while the Republic of Guinea had won its independence from France in 1958.

Amilcar Cabral was the central leader of the liberation movement in Guinea-Bissau and Cape Verde, and because of his knowledge of Africa, he made a big impression on me. Che had held a high opinion of the PAIGC (African Party for the Independence of Guinea and Cape Verde). At that time Che considered it a serious and organized revolutionary movement.

I arrived in Guinea-Bissau with the experience I had gained

in the Congo and a little more knowledge about Africa.

From a strategic point of view, Amilcar and I didn't always share the same opinion on how to wage the struggle. But you have to remember that it's the leaders within each country who must decide the form to carry out the struggle.

I'll give an example.

One day the liberation movement in Guinea-Bissau decided to recruit a group of young people. They went into a small town and took six young men and brought them to the camp. I didn't understand this. How can you compel people to join? I said this to Amilcar. "You can't force people to fight," I told him. "You must win them over politically."

Amilcar listened to me very respectfully. Keep in mind he had lots of experience and I was a young person—not yet thirty—and new to that country. "Everything you're saying is true," he said to me. "But here that can't be done. Because tomorrow the Portuguese will come, and they'll forcibly take them away and conscript them to fight against us. We have to incorporate them into our ranks before the Portuguese do."

Another question was that of the neighboring Republic of Guinea, with its capital in Conakry. The command of the PAIGC was in Guinea-Conakry. Why? Because there were only two ways to enter Guinea-Bissau: through Senegal—which gave no assistance at all—or Guinea-Conakry, whose government was then headed by Sékou Touré. Without that rear guard, the armed struggle in Guinea-Bissau would have been wiped out, since food supplies, armaments, and ammunition, which came from Cuba, China, the Soviet Union, and other socialist countries had to go through that country.

This was different from the struggle in our country, where our weapons were captured from the dictatorship's army. The Portuguese remained in their garrisons and rarely came out to fight. So you couldn't set ambushes to attack them and seize their weapons. They moved troops, supplies, everything, by plane and helicopter. The liberation movement needed a secure rear guard in order to survive.

That's why in November 1970, the Portuguese imperialists decided on an operation directly attacking Guinea-Conakry, trying to overthrow Sékou Touré while simultaneously trying to wipe out the liberation movement in Guinea-Bissau. That invasion was defeated by militias trained by Cuban instructors.

The Cuban leadership supported the strategy of strengthening the government of Sékou Touré. He asked for our help. We had to prevent the imperialists from toppling his government. We also knew that the French imperialists still didn't forgive Sékou Touré or the liberation movement for winning independence a few years earlier.

So Cuba responded to the request by Sékou Touré for Cuban instructors to help create a militia. We also respnded to a proposal by Amilcar Cabral to help train artillery personnel and doctors to meet the needs of the people of Guinea-Bissau, sending a small military unit. We taught them the use of artillery and trained them to give medical care to the liberation fighters.

We lived together with these compañeros in the same camps. This brought us even closer to the African struggle, and it enabled us to appreciate and to better understand the African people. And at the same time, they made an effort to understand us.

By the time of Guinea-Bissau's victory in 1974, I was no longer there. But later I began to work in Cape Verde, as well as in other countries such as the Congo-Brazzaville. These governments requested Cuba to train people in medicine and other specialties, and we also trained their armed forces. I took part in all that.

In 1969–70 I was head and deputy head of the Political Directorate of the Revolutionary Armed Forces. One of our responsibilities was to work with Africans, as well as working to prepare Cubans for internationalist missions in Africa.

As vice president of the Cuba-Africa Friendship Association, I've had relations with Africans from all countries on the continent, not just those I've been to as a combatant or a worker. Because, as I said, many Africans come to Cuba to study. At first we set up a school, where the teachers were all Cuban compañeros who had been in Africa. I was the director of that school. Later on, many of the teachers came from these countries.

I also got to know many Angolan compañeros, even though I didn't participate in that struggle.

In 1990 I returned to civilian life, but I've maintained my ties to Africa. I've headed up work in Africa for ANTEX and then UNECA, Cuban enterprises involved in trade and construction. I've been sent on missions to numerous African countries, negotiating projects that would help these countries—this time from the point of view of construction and health care.

In this capacity I've had the opportunity to live in some of these countries, such as Ghana, the Republic of Guinea, and the Congo. In each I spent one or more years helping to build housing.

Today I work for UNECA with responsibilities for Central Africa. My job is to work with those countries on construction projects, reconstruction of countries that have been destroyed by wars. We build housing, roads, and other things.

WATERS: At the World Youth Festival in Algeria this past summer, young people who went from the United States, France, Britain, and other imperialist countries noted that African young people there were eagerly seeking information on their history. They wanted books by revolutionary leaders like Thomas Sankara of Burkina Faso, as well as Che and Fidel. Unlike earlier generations, it's not just a question of fighting for independence from the colonial master. The vanguard of the new generation is seeking to prepare the necessary conditions of struggle against imperialist domination in all the forms it takes today.

DREKE: I agree. Within Africa there's a different response from what it was back then. The times are also different. There's a political struggle. It's not simply an armed struggle for national liberation, like the just struggle the people of Africa had to wage in the 1960s.

The people of Africa are not political novices. I know this because many Africans have come to study in Cuba. I've often had the opportunity to exchange ideas with them and listen to their opinions. And the views they express are very clear.

What are some of my conclusions?

For one thing, of the parties in Africa that I'm familiar with, there are none I would venture to call Marxist or Leninist. They're deeply nationalist; that's what they are. There are still places where nationalism has not yet taken root, where tribal or ethnic divisions continue to prevail. That's where imperialism seeks to intervene, sowing divisions among the people of Africa. And whenever a leader emerges who to a greater or lesser degree fights for independence or sovereignty and has a following, it seems they often die in an "accident" or through an assassination attempt. Sometimes they even just "disappear."

Then you see all these conflicts. There are countries that have been at war for years. One of the most important steps forward recently is that Africans are coming to a clearer understanding that internecine wars lead only to internal destruction. I'm not talking about wars for independence, sovereignty, and liberation. That's something entirely different.

One very big battle they are waging, as you know, is the battle against AIDS and other terrible diseases that afflict these peoples. Our doctors are making a great effort in this war. In Equatorial Guinea, South Africa, and other countries, there are Cuban doctors working. Some compañeros were in Africa earlier as combatants in wars of liberation; now they're serving there as doctors.

That's why I think it's true that there is a great movement in Africa of people seeking to read, to study, to learn their true history.

WATERS: What has been the impact here in Cuba of the fact that hundreds of thousands of Cubans—a high percentage of the population—have participated in internationalist missions in Africa over the last thirty years?

DREKE: The thousands of Cuban compañeros who have been fighting, or working in health care, in education, in sports, or in other areas in Africa, have brought back knowledge to Cuba. Cuba and Africa have influenced each other deeply. Our doctors have brought back experience in treating diseases they had read about but never seen; these experiences have helped save lives there, in other countries, and then even here in Cuba. Our doctors have worked in the most difficult places, they've taken care of the people, and they've won their affection. But in addition to those kinds of things, the Cuban people have also developed real affection and respect for their African brothers and sisters.

It's important to tell the truth. There was a stage, at the very beginning, when some people in Cuba didn't feel this way about Africa. What was said about Africans was not always good. Back then, any black African was called "Congo." It didn't matter if they were from Tanzania or wherever.

But most of the hundreds of thousands of our compañeros who have returned feel like they've left part of their family there. Whenever someone comes back from a visit to an African country, compañeros here ask: "How's so-and-so doing?" "How's his aunt, who took care of me when I was sick?" A brotherhood has developed between Cubans and Africans.

Within Africa, too, there's a lot of sympathy and respect for Cuba and for Fidel, and for the Cuban compañeros who served in internationalist missions on that continent.

Through our experiences in Africa, we saw firsthand the extreme poverty in which a great part of humanity lives. We've learned more about imperialist exploitation. It's not only that you've read something about the exploitation of man by man in a book by Karl Marx or Lenin. You've seen it, you've lived it concretely.

We say we have African blood in our veins, and you see this in Cuba every day, with our dance, our music, everything. It doesn't matter whether your skin color is lighter or darker. There's an African presence in all of us.

Fidel Castro and the revolution have taught us to identify ourselves deeply with our ties to Africa and to appreciate them. The presence of so many of our compañeros in Africa has played a big role making it possible for us to internalize this appreciation.

Glossary

Abrantes, Juan (The Mexican) (1935–1959) – Joined the Revolutionary Directorate while a student at the University of Havana. During 1958 he became a captain in the Revolutionary Directorate column in Escambray mountains commanded by Faure Chomón. During 1959, having advanced to the rank of commander, he became head of the Rebel Army's Tactical Forces in Las Villas and Matanzas. Killed in airplane crash, September 1959.

Acosta, Armando (1920–) – A member of the PSP; he formed guerrilla detachment in Escambray mountains, collaborating with Che Guevara. Became a captain in the Rebel Army and was promoted to commander. General secretary of Communist Party in Oriente province until 1966. Later served as national coordinator of CDRs. A member of Communist Party Central Committee 1965–91.

Alarcón, Dariel (Benigno) (1939–) – Peasant from Cuba's Sierra Maestra. Joined Rebel Army July 1957, serving under Camilo Cienfuegos. After the revolution's triumph, he continued working in armed forces, reaching the rank of lieutenant in the Cuban army. He was a combatant in Bolivia with Che in 1966–67. One of three surviving Cuban veterans of the guerrilla front who escaped and reached Cuba in March 1968. Retired from the Ministry of Interior in 1979 with rank of lieutenant colonel. He left Cuba in 1996, making wildly false attacks on the revolution and its leadership.

Almeida, Juan (1927–) – A bricklayer from Havana and a member of the Orthodox Party at the time of Batista's 1952 coup, he was recruited to the movement led by Fidel Castro and participated in the 1953 Moncada attack; sentenced to ten years in prison. Released with the

153

other Moncada prisoners in May 1955 following a national amnesty campaign, he participated in the *Granma* expedition of November–December 1956. In February 1958 he was promoted to commander and later headed the Third Eastern Front. Almeida has carried numerous responsibilities since 1959, including head of the air force, vice minister of the Revolutionary Armed Forces, and vice president of the Council of Ministers. He has been a member of the Communist Party Central Committee and Political Bureau since 1965. Currently president of the Association of Combatants of the Cuban Revolution.

Alpha 66 – Armed organization of Cuban counterrevolutionaries based in the United States. It was set up in 1961, with Washington's support, to carry out acts of sabotage primarily against economic targets in Cuba. It also claimed responsibility for numerous acts of terror in Miami, New York, San Juan, and elsewhere. In the late 1990s it claimed responsibility for bomb attacks on several hotels in Havana, in which one person was killed.

Ameijeiras, Efigenio (1931–) – Joined the revolutionary struggle against the Batista regime in March 1952. A *Granma* expeditionary in 1956, he finished the war as commander of Rebel Army Column 6 and second in command of the Second Eastern Front. Head of the Revolutionary National Police and of its battalion that fought at Playa Girón in April 1961. In 1963 he commanded the Cuban internationalist contingent in Algeria. In 1984 he went to Angola, where he served as a leader of Cuba's volunteer mission. Currently a division general in Cuban armed forces.

Aragonés, Emilio (1928–) – A leader of the July 26 Movement in Cienfuegos during the insurrectional struggle, he became its national coordinator in 1960. In March 1962 he was elected to the National Directorate and Secretariat of the Integrated Revolutionary Organization (ORI). He was a member of the Communist Party's Central Committee 1965–91. In September 1965 he participated in a delegation sent to the Congo by the leadership of the party to consult and work with Che Guevara.

Arias Echenique, Mario (1924–1997) – Coordinator of the Revolutionary Directorate in Sagua la Grande during the late 1950s.

Ascunce, Manuel (1945–1961) – Literacy brigadista and member of Association of Rebel Youth. Together with a peasant he was teaching, Ascunce was tortured and hanged in the Escambray mountains November 26, 1961, by counterrevolutionary bandits Julio Emilio Carretero, Pedro González, and Braulio Quesada.

Association of Rebel Youth. See Union of Young Communists (UJC)

Authentic Organization – Military organization set up by leaders of the Authentic Party to oppose Batista following his 1952 coup.

Authentic Party (Cuban Revolutionary Party) – Bourgeois-nationalist party popularly known as *auténticos*. The party was formed in 1934, claiming to be authentic followers of José Martí's Cuban Revolutionary Party. The party held the presidency from 1944 until 1952, under Ramón Grau and then Carlos Prío. It was one of the main components of the bourgeois opposition to Batista in 1952–58. After the Batista regime fell, as the revolution deepened during 1959–60, the leaders of the Authentic Party left Cuba for the U.S., where they joined the counterrevolutionary forces.

Batista, Fulgencio (1901–1973) – Former army sergeant who helped lead a military coup by junior officers in September 1933, in the wake of a popular uprising that had overturned the dictatorship of Gerardo Machado a few weeks earlier. He rose to chief of staff and, in January 1934, organized a second coup that unleashed a reign of repression against workers, peasants, and revolutionary forces. After dominating several governments as army chief of staff, Batista was elected president in 1940. He stepped aside from office in the 1944 elections, but retained a base of support within the army officer corps, living in Florida until 1948. Batista led a coup on March 10, 1952, establishing a brutal military dictatorship that collaborated closely with Washington. He fled to the Dominican Republic on January 1, 1959.

Ben Bella, Ahmed (1918–) – Leader of the National Liberation Front (FLN) of Algeria, which mobilized the Algerian people in the 1954–62 struggle for independence from France. He was president of the workers and peasants government that came to power following the victory over Paris in 1962 and collaborated closely with the Cuban government to advance anti-imperialist struggles in Africa and Latin America. He was overthrown in a coup led by defense minister Col.

Houari Boumedienne in June 1965.

Benigno. See Alarcón, Dariel

Benítez, Conrado (1942–1961) – Volunteer literacy teacher in the Escambray mountains tortured and hanged by counterrevolutionary bandits January 5, 1961, together with peasant Eliodoro Rodríguez Linares.

Bordón, Víctor (1930–) – Member of Orthodox Youth and later July 26 Movement in Las Villas. He formed a July 26 Movement guerrilla unit in Las Villas in late 1956 that became part of Che Guevara's column in October 1958. Attained rank of Rebel Army commander. Later worked in Ministry of Construction in Matanzas.

Boumedienne, Houari (1932–1978) – A leader of the Algerian Army of National Liberation (ALN) in the independence war against France. Minister of defense in the revolutionary government established by the National Liberation Front (FLN) following independence in 1962. He led a coup that overthrew the workers and farmers government of Ahmed Ben Bella in June 1965. He was president of Algeria 1965–78.

Bravo, Mario (d. 1964) – Counterrevolutionary bandit in the Escambray. Killed in battle June 1964.

Cabral, Amilcar (1924–1973) – Founder and central leader of the African Party for the Independence of Guinea-Bissau and Cape Verde (PAIGC), 1956, which in 1963 took up arms against Portuguese colonial rule, winning independence of Guinea-Bissau in 1974 and Cape Verde in 1975. He was assassinated in January 1973.

Campos, Benito (Campito) (d. 1964) – Captain in Rebel Army who broke with the revolution and became a leader of counterrevolutionary band in Escambray. Killed in battle September 1964.

Campos, José Martí (Campito) (d. 1964) – A bandit leader in the Escambray, he was the son of Benito Campos. Killed in battle September 1964.

Carreras, Jesús (d. 1961) – A leader of Second National Front of the Escambray. He joined armed counterrevolutionary bands in Escambray after the revolution's victory. Captured, tried, and executed in March 1961.

Carretero, Julio Emilio (d. 1964) – Member of Batista's secret police during the dictatorship. Counterrevolutionary bandit in the Escambray beginning in 1960. One of the murderers of literacy brigadista Manuel Ascunce in November 1961. In early 1963 he became head of all counterrevolutionary bands in the Escambray. Captured, tried, and executed in June 1964.

Castelló, Humberto (1922–) – A member of the Revolutionary Directorate, he participated in the March 13, 1957, attack on the Presidential Palace and Radio Reloj. Later became a commander in the Revolutionary Directorate guerrilla column in the Escambray. A medical doctor by profession.

Castellón, Gustavo (Mayaguara Horse) – Peasant and miner from Fomento area in Las Villas. Joined Revolutionary Directorate column in Escambray in 1958. Member of the Ramón Pando Ferrer Commando Unit, he fought in the battle of Santa Clara. One of Cuba's most renowned "bandit hunters" in the Escambray in the early to mid-1960s, he headed a special LCB company. He later carried out an internationalist mission in Angola.

Castro, Fidel (1926–) – A student leader at the University of Havana from 1945 on, he was the central organizer of Orthodox Party youth after party founding in 1947. He was an Orthodox Party candidate for House of Representatives in the 1952 elections canceled by Batista following the coup in March of that year. In 1953 Castro organized a new revolutionary movement that came to be known as the Centennial Generation, named in honor of the 100th anniversary of José Martí's birth, to carry out the struggle against the Batista dictatorship. He organized and led the July 1953 attack on the Moncada garrison. Captured, tried, and sentenced to fifteen years in prison, his courtroom defense speech, "History Will Absolve Me," was distributed in tens of thousands of copies across Cuba, becoming the program of the revolutionary movement. Released in 1955 after a mass amnesty campaign, Castro led the founding of the July 26 Revolutionary Movement. He organized the *Granma* expedition from Mexico in late 1956 and commanded the Rebel Army during the revolutionary war; he became general secretary of the July 26 Movement in May 1958. Following the triumph of the revolution, Castro was Cuba's prime minister from February 1959 to 1976, and has been president of the Council of State and Council of Ministers since then. He is commander in chief of the Revolutionary Armed Forces and, since 1965, the first secretary of the Communist Party of Cuba.

Castro, Raúl (1931–) – A participant in student protests against the Batista dictatorship, he joined in the 1953 Moncada attack and was sentenced to thirteen years in prison. He was released in May 1955 following a national amnesty campaign. A founding member of the July 26 Movement, he was a participant in the 1956 *Granma* expedition and a founding member of the Rebel Army. In February 1958 he was promoted to commander and headed the Second Eastern Front. Since October 1959 he has been minister of the Revolutionary Armed Forces. He is General of the Army, the second-ranking officer of the Revolutionary Armed Forces. He was vice premier from 1959 until 1976, when he became first vice president of the Council of State and Council of Ministers. Since 1965 he has been second secretary of the Communist Party of Cuba.

Castro, Osvaldo Lorenzo (Pineo) – Head of LCB in the mid-1960s. Currently a brigadier general in the Revolutionary Armed Forces.

CDRs. See Committees for the Defense of the Revolution

Chomón, Faure (1929–) – Leader of Revolutionary Directorate and survivor of March 13, 1957, attack on Presidential Palace. He organized a February 1958 expedition landing in northern Camagüey that established a guerrilla front in the Escambray mountains. Was part of the Las Villas front under Che Guevara's command after the latter's column arrived in October. On behalf of the Revolutionary Directorate, he signed the Pedrero Pact at the beginning of December. Chomón holds the rank of commander in the Revolutionary Armed Forces and has been a member of the Communist Party Central Committee since 1965. He has served as Cuba's ambassador to the Soviet Union, Vietnam, and Ecuador.

Choy, Armando (1934–) – Member of Rebel Army during Cuba's revolutionary war, he was promoted to captain by Che Guevara. He was a leader of Cuba's antiaircraft defenses. In 1976 he became a brigadier general in the Revolutionary Armed Forces. Currently delegate of the Ministry of Transportation to the Maritime Port Operations, and president of the Working Group for the Conservation and Development of Havana Bay.

Cienfuegos, Camilo (1932–1959) – An opponent of the 1952 Batista coup, Cienfuegos lived in the U.S. in 1953–54, working in garment shops and restaurants in New York, San Francisco, and Chicago before being arrested and deported by U.S. immigration cops. In 1956 he went to Mexico to enlist in the armed struggle against Batista. A *Granma* expeditionary, he became a captain in Che Guevara's Rebel Army column in late 1957. He was promoted to commander in 1958 and led the "Antonio Maceo" Column 2 westward on an invasion from Sierra Maestra en route to Pinar del Río from August to October 1958. He operated in northern Las Villas until the end of the war and became Rebel Army chief of staff in January 1959. He was killed when his plane was lost at sea while returning to Havana on October 28, 1959.

Cienfuegos, Osmany (1931–) – A member of the Socialist Youth, affiliated with the Popular Socialist Party, during Cuba's revolutionary war. He served as minister of public works 1959–63 and minister of construction 1963–66. He has been a member of the Communist Party Central Committee since 1965, and is a vice president of the Executive Committee of the Council of Ministers. He is the older brother of Camilo Cienfuegos.

Committees for the Defense of the Revolution (CDRs) – Organized in 1960 on a block-by-block basis as a tool through which the Cuban people could exercise vigilance against counterrevolutionary activity. In subsequent years they have also served as a vehicle to organize participation at mass demonstrations and to take part in vaccination and other public health campaigns, civil defense, the fight against petty crime, and other civic tasks.

Cubela, Rolando (1933–) – A leader of Revolutionary Directorate guerrilla column in the Escambray mountains. He headed the Federation of University Students 1959–60. As attaché to Cuban embassy in Madrid in 1963, he was recruited by the CIA to assassinate Fidel Castro in a plot also involving Manuel Artime, a politician who played a role in the defeated April 1961 invasion at the Bay of Pigs. Cubela was captured and sentenced to twenty-five years in prison in 1966. After being released in 1979, he moved to Spain.

Delgado, Alberto (The Man of Maisinicú) (d. 1964) – Member of Cuban State Security who successfully infiltrated counterrevolutionary bands. His base of operations was a farm in Maisinicú in the Escambray. In March 1964 he took central responsibility for arranging a ruse in which one of the last bands believed it was escaping by boat to the U.S. but was instead captured at sea. He was lynched by counterrevolutionaries in April 1964 after they figured out his role in the operation.

de los Santos, René (1918–) – Combatant of the Rebel Army; a commander of one of the fronts at Playa Girón coming from the east. He was a member of the Central Committee of the Communist Party of Cuba 1975–86.

Denis, Luis Felipe – Lieutenant working for Cuban State Security in the struggle against bandits in the Escambray.

Duque, Evelio – Peasant from the Escambray. His brother was a member of the Revolutionary Directorate, and he passed himself off as a Directorate member. After 1959 he became a notorious bandit in the Escambray. In December 1960 he became head of the bandits' umbrella organization, which they called the Army of National Liberation (ELN). Went into exile in U.S., where, working under the CIA, he continued organizing armed counterrevolutionary raids against Cuba.

Echeverría, José Antonio (1932–1957) – President of Federation of University Students from 1954 until his death. He was the central leader of Revolutionary Directorate; killed March 13, 1957, in Directorate-organized attack on the Presidential Palace and Radio Reloj, whose goal was the assassination of Batista.

Escalona, Dermidio – Joined Rebel Army June 1957 and became a combatant in the First Front, led by Fidel Castro. He was assigned to open a new front in the Órganos mountains in Pinar del Río in May 1958, ending the war with rank of commander. For a period beginning in late 1960 he commanded the struggle against counterrevolutionary bandits.

Fajardo, Manuel (Piti) (1930–1960) – Joined Rebel Army in 1958 as doctor and combatant in Columns 1 and 12, reaching rank of commander. The first head of what later became the Lucha Contra Bandidos, he was killed in combat against counterrevolutionary forces in Escambray mountains November 29, 1960.

Federation of Cuban Women (FMC) – Founded August 23, 1960, with Rebel Army combatant Vilma Espín as its president, it united pro-revolutionary women's organizations. It has sought to integrate women into the revolution's tasks and the work force, while championing the fight for women's equality in society.

Figueredo, Idelfredo (Chino) (1930–) – Combatant in Rebel Army Columns 1 and 4. Promoted to captain and named head of column in Rebel Army's Camagüey Front. Participated in the battle of Santa Clara. Currently a colonel in the Revolutionary Armed Forces no longer on active duty.

Fleites, Roberto (d. 1958) – From a poor family, he was a member of the Revolutionary Directorate guerrilla column in the Escambray and a member of the Ramón Pando Ferrer commando squad. He participated in the rescue of Directorate combatant Joaquín Milanés, and was killed in the battle of Santa Clara.

García, Calixto (1931–) – Participated in July 26, 1953, attack on Bayamo garrison; escaped and went to Costa Rica, Honduras, and Mexico. Met Ernesto Guevara in Costa Rica in November 1953. A *Granma* expeditionary, he finished the revolutionary war as a Rebel Army commander on the Third Front. He was later head of the Eastern and Central Armies and held other military posts in the FAR and Communist Party. A member of the Communist Party Central Committee 1965–80. Currently a brigadier general in the Cuban armed forces.

Gómez Ochoa, Delio (1929–) – Rebel Army fighter; after failure of April 1958 general strike, he became July 26 Movement national action coordinator, based in Havana. A Rebel Army commander, he became head of the Fourth Eastern Front six months later, in October. He led an armed expedition to the Dominican Republic in June 1959 of Dominican and Cuban volunteers to fight the Trujillo dictatorship; he was captured and later released. He subsequently had responsibilities in the agricultural sector of Cuba's economy.

González Coro, Ramón (Mongo) (1931–1958) – Joined the Revolutionary Directorate guerrilla front in the Escambray as a medical student. A captain in the column, heading the José Antonio Sanchidrian commando squad. Killed during the rescue of jailed Directorate combatant Joaquín Milanés in Santa Clara, December 1958.

González, Pedro (d. 1964) – Member of Batista army during revolutionary war and served in the Sierra Maestra under the notorious murderer Col. Angel Sánchez Mosquera. Counterrevolutionary bandit in the Escambray. One of the murderers of literacy brigadista Manuel Ascunce in November 1961. Killed in battle October 1964.

Guevara, Ernesto Che (1928–1967) – Argentine-born leader of the Cuban Revolution. A participant in the *Granma* expedition and a founding member of the Rebel Army, he was the first combatant to be promoted to the rank of commander during Cuba's revolutionary war. In late 1958 he united various revolutionary organizations in central Cuba under his command and led them in the capture of Santa Clara, the island's third most important city. Following the 1959 triumph, in addition to his military tasks, Guevara held a number of positions and responsibilities in the revolutionary government including head of the National Bank and minister of industry; he often represented the revolutionary leadership internationally. In April 1965 he led the Cuban column that fought for several months alongside anti-imperialist forces in the Congo. In late 1966 he led a vanguard detachment of internationalist volunteers to Bolivia. Wounded and captured by the Bolivian army in a CIA-organized operation on October 8, 1967, he was murdered the following day.

Guillén, Porfirio (d. 1963) – Counterrevolutionary bandit in the Escambray. Killed in battle outside Manicaragua, January 1963.

Guiteras, Antonio (1906–1935) – Student leader of struggles against the dictatorship of Gerardo Machado in 1920s and 1930s. A leader of anti-imperialist forces during the 1933 revolutionary upsurge that overthrew the Machado regime, he became interior minister in the Hundred Days Government brought to power by that upsurge in September 1933 and overthrown in January 1934 in a coup by Batista. Guiteras was murdered in January 1935, as he was leading the clandestine struggle against the regime.

Gutiérrez Menoyo, Eloy (1934–) – Leader of the Second National Front of the Escambray in 1958, which was expelled from the Revolutionary Directorate for its conduct toward the peasantry and its close ties to bourgeois forces in the anti-Batista opposition. He left Cuba for United States in 1960 and returned with a counterrevolutionary armed band in December 1964. Captured and imprisoned until 1986. Currently head of Miami-based organization Cambio Cubano (Cuban Change).

Hundred Days Government – In September 1933, in the wake of the revolutionary upsurge that overthrew the dictatorship of Gerardo Machado the previous month, a coup by junior officers led by Fulgencio Batista established a coalition government led by Ramón Grau San Martín. The new government included revolutionary forces, among them Antonio Guiteras, who became minister of the interior. During this period, some of the demands long fought for by working people were realized, such as annulment of the U.S.-imposed Platt Amendment, the eight-hour day, and women's suffrage. In January 1934 Batista carried out a second coup with U.S. backing and put an end to the Hundred Days Government, installing a regime compliant to capitalist interests in the United States and Cuba. Batista, who had been appointed head of the army and dominated the new government, sought to buy off former opponents of the Machado dictatorship, while carrying out murderous repression against those who refused to buckle, such as Guiteras.

Ilanga, Freddy (1948–) – Member of the Congolese anti-imperialist forces. Worked with the Cuban contingent in 1965. In November of that year he accompanied combatants back to Cuba, where he became a doctor.

July 26 Revolutionary Movement – Founded June 1955 by Fidel Castro and other veterans of Moncada attack, along with youth activists from the left wing of the Orthodox Party and other forces, including the National Revolutionary Action led by Frank País in Santiago and veterans of the Revolutionary National Movement such as Armando Hart and Faustino Pérez in Havana. The July 26 Movement separated from the Orthodox Party in March 1956. During the revolutionary war it was composed of the Rebel Army in the mountains *(Sierra)* and the urban underground network *(Llano)*. Fidel Castro became general secretary of the movement in May 1958. It began publishing *Revolución* during the revolutionary war. Following the victory the July 26 Movement fused in 1961 with the Popular Socialist Party and Revolutionary Directorate to form the Integrated Revolutionary Organizations and later the Communist Party of Cuba.

Kabila, Laurent-Désiré (1939–2001) – Leader of the Congolese youth movement under Patrice Lumumba. He opposed the 1960 Belgian- and U.S.-backed coup that brought down the anti-imperialist government of the newly independent country, headed by Lumumba. Kabila helped lead the 1964 rebellion against the pro-imperialist regime of Joseph Kasavubu and Moise Tshombe. He was a leader of the Congolese forces assisted in 1965 by the Cuban internationalist column headed by Che Guevara. He founded the People's Revolutionary Party in 1967. Following the ouster of the Mobutu dictatorship in 1997, Kabila became the country's head of state. He was assassinated in January 2001.

Lara, Luis (d. 1959) – Former corporal in the Batista army, he was taken prisoner after the victory of the revolution. He escaped and went to the mountains of Pinar del Río, where he organized the first counterrevolutionary guerrilla band, responsible for over 20 murders. He was captured, tried, and executed in December 1959.

LCB. See Lucha Contra Bandidos

López Pardo, Raúl (Raulín) (1943–1965) – From a poor family of fishermen in Havana. He joined the Revolutionary Directorate guerrilla front in the Escambray. Participant in the rescue of jailed Revolutionary Directorate combatant Joaquín Milanés in Santa Clara, December 1958. A first lieutenant in the Revolutionary Armed Forces.

Lucha Contra Bandidos (LCB) – Formed July 3, 1962, as a special command in the Central Army of the Revolutionary Armed Forces to combat counterrevolutionary groups. It was discontinued after the victory over the bandits, with many of its cadres becoming part of a new command called Lucha Contra Piratas (struggle against pirates), to stop counterrevolutionary infiltrations by sea.

Lumumba, Patrice (1925–1961) – Leader of the independence struggle in the Congo and prime minister after independence from Belgium in June 1960. In September 1960, after requesting United Nations troops to block attacks by Belgian-backed mercenaries, his govern-

ment was overthrown in a coup instigated by Belgium and the U.S.
UN troops supposedly guarding Lumumba took no action as he and
two associates were captured and jailed. They were then turned over
to the Katanga secessionist government of Moise Tshombe and murdered in January 1961.

Machado Ventura, José R. (Machadito) (1930–) – Member of the July
26 Movement and a medical doctor, he joined the Rebel Army during the revolutionary war and served under Raúl Castro, attaining
the rank of commander. He was minister of public health 1960–68,
and first secretary of the Havana provincial committee of the Communist Party 1971–76. He has been a member of the Central Committee of the Communist Party since 1965. A long-time member of
the Political Bureau, he has been on the Central Committee Secretariat since 1976. He is a member of the Council of State.

Machín, Gustavo (1937–1967) – Active in the movement against Batista at the University of Havana, and a leader of the Revolutionary
Directorate. In February 1958 he helped organize the landing of a
Directorate guerrilla column, which established a base in the Escambray mountains. In December 1958 he fought in the battle of Santa
Clara under Guevara's command, ending the war with the rank of
commander. Machín held a number of government posts after 1959,
including vice minister of industry, before returning to active military duty. Under the nom-de-guerre Alejandro, he served as head
of operations in the revolutionary front in Bolivia in 1966–67; he was
responsible for planning and coordination of military logistics. He
was killed in battle in August 1967.

Man of Maisinicú. See Delgado, Alberto

Martí, José (1853–1895) – A noted revolutionary, poet, writer, speaker,
and journalist, he is Cuba's national hero. He founded the Cuban
Revolutionary Party in 1892 to fight Spanish colonial rule and oppose U.S. designs on Cuba. He organized and planned the 1895 independence war and was killed in battle at Dos Ríos in Oriente province. His revolutionary anti-imperialist program is part of the
internationalist traditions and political heritage of the Cuban Revolution.

Martínez Andrade, Juan Alberto (d. 1965) – A counterrevolutionary bandit in the Escambray from 1961. He led one of the last bands and was killed in battle July 7, 1965.

Martínez Tamayo, José María (Papi) (1936–1967) – Known also by the noms-de-guerre of Mbili and Ricardo. Worked as Guevara's liaison with revolutionary forces in Latin America beginning in 1962. Served with Guevara in the Congo and then Bolivia, where he was in charge of the advance preparations for the guerrilla front. He was killed in battle in June 1967.

Masferrer, Rolando (1914–1975) – A pro-Batista senator and wealthy bourgeois politician. In the 1950s he organized and led a private paramilitary squad of some 2,000 torturers, assassins, and extortionists known as the "Tigers." In the 1930s Masferrer had been a member of the Cuban Communist Party (which took the name Popular Socialist Party in 1944) and fought as a volunteer in the Spanish civil war, leaving the party in 1945. He fled Cuba December 31, 1958. Masferrer was killed by a car bomb in Miami in a gangland hit sixteen years later.

Mayaguara Horse. See Castellón, Gustavo

Menéndez, Jesús (1911–1948) – General secretary of the National Federation of Sugar Workers and a leader of the Popular Socialist Party. He was murdered at the Manzanillo train station by police captain Joaquín Casillas in January 1948.

Menéndez Tomassevich, Raúl (Tomás) (1929–2001) – Won to the July 26 Movement while in prison, he helped organize a jailbreak on November 30, 1956, as part of the uprising in Santiago led by Frank País timed to coincide with the *Granma* landing. He fought in the urban underground, and in May 1957 joined the Rebel Army, where he became a captain in the Second Eastern Front led by Raúl Castro. He led Cuba's 117th Battalion at the Bay of Pigs. In 1962 he became head of Lucha Contra Bandidos special forces. In 1966 he helped organize Cuban volunteers to aid the forces in Guinea-Bissau fighting for independence from Portugal. He participated in a guerrilla movement in Venezuela in 1967. He served three tours of duty in Angola in the 1970s and 1980s, twice as head of the Cuban military mission. A member of Communist Party Central Committee from 1965 on, he was a division general at the time of his death.

Milanés Olivares, Joaquín (The Magnificent) – Member of the Revolutionary Directorate involved in the unsuccessful attempt to assassinate Batista minister Santiago Rey in Havana, June 13, 1958. Arrested in Sancti Spíritus, he was freed in a commando raid in Santa Clara, December 17, 1958. Designated leader of the Ramón González Coro Commando Unit with the rank of captain, he participated in the battle for the liberation of Trinidad, December 28–31, 1958.

Morejón, Julián – Company chief in LCB. Later served as a member of the Cuban contingent in the Congo under Che.

Morgan, William (d. 1961) – A former member of the U.S. army, he became a leader of the Second National Front of the Escambray. Following the fall of the dictatorship, he set up a frog farm near Trinidad, which he used to channel supplies to the counterrevolutionary bands in the Escambray, before joining them himself. He was captured, tried, and executed in March 1961.

Moja – Víctor Dreke's nom-de-guerre in the Congo.

National Association of Small Farmers (ANAP) – Organization of Cuban farmers founded 1961. Aids and represents farmers working privately held land and members of farming cooperatives.

Nieves, Raúl (1936–) – An industrial worker, he was a prominent member of the Orthodox Youth. He was a commander in the Revolutionary Directorate column in the Escambray in 1958. As head of the Ramón Pando Ferrer commando unit, he led the attack on Squadron 31 during the battle of Santa Clara. After the revolution's victory, he was named chief of police in Cienfuegos. He next served in the army's general inspection unit, and then worked with Che Guevara in the Department of Industrialization of the National Institute for Agrarian Reform (INRA). Later worked in the Ministry of Transportation.

Olaechea, Catalino – Lieutenant in Lucha Contra Bandidos. Served as company commander in the Cuban contingent in the Congo under Che in 1965.

Oliva, Rogelio – Cuban revolutionary assigned to the Cuban embassy in Tanzania in November 1963. From Tanzania in 1965, he was assigned to maintain contact between Che's column and Cuba.

Organization of African Unity (OAU) – Founded May 1963 in Ethiopia by thirty-two African states. Its charter called for an end to colonialism and for independence and sovereignty for all of Africa. During 1964–65 the OAU gave support to the struggle in the Congo against the neocolonial regime, withdrawing that support in November 1965. The OAU currently includes virtually all governments in Africa.

Orthodox Party (Cuban People's Party) – Known as the *ortodoxos,* this party was formed in 1947 on a platform of opposition to U.S. domination of Cuba and government corruption. Its youth wing provided many of the initial cadres for the Moncada assault. Its leadership moved rightward after Batista's 1952 coup, and the party fragmented.

País, Frank (1934–1957) – Vice president of the Federation of University Students in Oriente, he was the central leader of Oriente Revolutionary Action, later renamed National Revolutionary Action, which fused with the Moncada veterans and other forces to form the July 26 Movement in 1955. He was the central leader of July 26 Movement in Oriente province, national action coordinator of the July 26 Movement, and head of its urban militias. He was murdered by the dictatorship's forces July 30, 1957.

Paneque, Víctor – Leader of the July 26 Movement in Las Villas during Cuba's revolutionary war. He left the country after the revolution's victory, becoming a leader of the counterrevolutionary Insurrectional Movement of Revolutionary Recuperation (MIRR).

Papi. See Martínez Tamayo, José María

Pardo Llada, José (1923–) – Radio announcer and Orthodox Party leader. Breaking with the *ortodoxos* in 1954, he participated in the Movement of the Nation and other activities organized by the bourgeois opposition to Batista. Continuing as a radio broadcaster after the revolution, he abandoned Cuba in March 1961.

Pazos, Felipe (1912–2001) – Head of the Cuban National Bank during Prío administration, he opposed Batista's 1952 coup. President of the National Bank, January–October 1959, he was replaced by Che Guevara. He opposed revolutionary measures and left Cuba for the U.S.

Peña, Lázaro (1911–1974) – Joined Communist Party in 1929. A leader of Popular Socialist Party before the revolution, he was general secretary of Cuba's trade union federation, 1939–49, 1961–66, 1973–74. A member of the Communist Party Central Committee at the time of his death.

Pinares. See Sánchez, Antonio

Piñeiro, Manuel (1933–1998) – A participant in student protests against Batista's 1952 coup, his family sent him to the United States in 1953, where he attended Columbia University and was deeply affected by the racism and social inequalities in the U.S. Returning to Cuba, he became a founding member of the July 26 Movement in 1955. He joined the Rebel Army in 1957 and fought in Raúl Castro's column during the revolutionary war. He was promoted to commander in January 1959. After the victory he helped organize State Security. In June 1961 he became deputy minister of the interior, as well as head of its Technical subministry responsible for coordinating Cuba's support to revolutionary movements around the world during the 1960s, including support for Che Guevara's columns in the Congo and Bolivia. In 1970 he became first vice minister of the Ministry of the Interior and head of its General Directorate of National Liberation. In 1975 he became head of the Communist Party's Department of the Americas, holding that position for 17 years. He was a member of the party's Central Committee from 1965 until 1997.

Pombo. See Villegas, Harry

Popular Socialist Party (PSP) – Name taken in 1944 by the Communist Party of Cuba. The PSP opposed the 1952 Batista coup and dictatorship but rejected the political course of the Moncada assault and of the July 26 Movement and Rebel Army in launching the revolutionary war in 1956–57. The PSP collaborated with the July 26 Movement in the final month of the struggle, with the aim of bringing down the Batista dictatorship. After the revolution's victory, the PSP fused with the July 26 Movement and Revolutionary Directorate in 1961 to form the Integrated Revolutionary Organizations, and later the Communist Party of Cuba in 1965.

Prieto, Plinio (1923–1960) – A member of the National Directorate of the Authentic Organization during the Batista dictatorship. In 1958 he joined the Second National Front of the Escambray. In June 1960 he went into armed rebellion against the revolution and helped organize a counterrevolutionary band in the Escambray, together with Sinesio Walsh. He was captured, tried, and executed in October 1960.

Prío Socarrás, Carlos (1903–1977) – Leader of the Authentic Party and president of Cuba from 1948 until Batista's 1952 coup. He was a leading figure in the bourgeois opposition during Cuba's revolutionary war. In early 1961 he left Cuba and went to the U.S.

Proenza, Lizardo (1926–1975) – From a peasant family in Oriente province, he joined the revolutionary struggle after Batista's coup. A member of the July 26 Movement in Bayamo, he survived a police attempt to assassinate him. He later joined a Rebel Army unit in Oriente and fought in the northern part of that province. Following the victory he was promoted to captain, and later became head of a unit in Lucha Contra Bandidos in Matanzas. He was in charge of all LCB operations in 1965.

Quesada, Ramón – A leader of a counterrevolutionary band in the Escambray. He left Cuba and returned in a CIA-organized landing led by Eloy Gutiérrez Menoyo in December 1964. Together with the other members of the band, he was captured, tried, and imprisoned.

Ramírez, Osvaldo (d. 1962) – A member of the Revolutionary Directorate guerrilla column during the revolutionary war, he became squadron chief in Caracusey after the victory. He later became a counterrevolutionary bandit in the Escambray. In January 1961 he became head of the bandits' umbrella organization, the Army of National Liberation (ELN). Killed in battle April 1962.

Revolutionary Directorate, March 13 – Formed in 1955 by José Antonio Echeverría and other leaders of the Federation of University Students. It organized an attack on the Presidential Palace and Radio Reloj on March 13, 1957, in which a number of central leaders, including Echeverría, were killed. The Directorate organized a guerrilla column in the Escambray mountains in Las Villas in February 1958 led by Faure Chomón. The Revolutionary Directorate fused with the July 26 Movement and PSP in 1961 to form the Integrated Revolutionary Organizations and later the Communist Party of Cuba.

Rey, Santiago (1910–) – Minister of interior in 1958 under the Batista dictatorship. He fled Cuba on January 1, 1959, and went to the Dominican Republic, where he later was a close adviser to Dominican president Joaquín Balaguer.

Reyes, Eliseo (San Luis) (1940–1967) – A native of San Luis in Cuba's Oriente province, he was active in the clandestine struggle against Batista and joined the Rebel Army in 1957, serving in Guevara's column and reaching the rank of captain. Following the triumph of the revolution he headed the military police at La Cabaña garrison in Havana, held military responsibilities in Las Villas, and became head of G-2, the counterintelligence division of Cuba's police. He was sent to Pinar del Río in 1962 to help lead operations against the counterrevolutionary bands, and was elected to the Central Committee of the Cuban Communist Party in October 1965. As a volunteer combatant, in 1966–67 he joined the revolutionary front in Bolivia led by Che Guevara, under the nom-de-guerre Rolando. A member of the front's general staff, he had responsibility for political leadership of the troops. He was killed in battle in April 1967.

Rivalta, Pablo (1926–) – A member of the Popular Socialist Party, he joined the Rebel Army in 1957 and became a captain, serving in Che Guevara's invasion column in 1958. In November 1963 he was assigned as Cuba's ambassador to Tanzania, where in 1965 he helped coordinate Cuba's support to the Congo column led by Guevara.

Rodríguez Sánchez, Conrado (1920–1997) – Leader of sugar workers union in Sagua la Grande in early 1950s and a supporter of the Authentic Party. He left Cuba for the United States after the victory of the revolution and joined with counterrevolutionary Cuban organizations in exile.

Sacerio, Roberto (1935–) – Founding member of the Revolutionary Directorate in Sagua la Grande. He joined its guerrilla front in the Escambray and was a member of the Ramón Pando Ferrer commando unit. He participated in the battle of Santa Clara.

Sánchez Arango, Aureliano (1907–1976) – Former student activist in the struggle against the 1925–33 Machado dictatorship, he later served as minister of education in the Carlos Prío government. During the Batista dictatorship he formed an organization called simply the AAA, which proclaimed its intention to wage armed struggle against the dictatorship but failed to do so. Following the victory of the revolution he engaged in counterrevolutionary activity and then fled to the U.S.

Sánchez, Antonio (Pinares) (1927–1967) – A native of Pinar del Río province in western Cuba, where he worked as a bricklayer. Went to the Sierra Maestra in early 1957 and after a three-month search succeeded in finding and joining the Rebel Army, becoming a captain and head of the rear guard in Camilo Cienfuegos's column. Promoted to commander on January 4, 1959. Subsequently held various posts in the armed forces, including head of operations in Pinar del Río, corps chief in Camagüey, and military commander on the Isle of Pines. Elected to the Central Committee of the Cuban Communist Party in October 1965. He joined the revolutionary front led by Che Guevara in Bolivia in November 1966 under the nom-de-guerre Marcos, and was killed in combat in June 1967.

San Luis. See Reyes, Eliseo

Santiago, Antonio (Tony) (1923–1961) – A native of Placetas in Las Villas, Santiago's parents sent him to the United States when he was 18. He joined the U.S. Navy during the Second World War, seeing combat in the Pacific. Returning to Cuba after the war, he went into exile in the United States after Batista's 1952 coup. Joining the revolutionary movement as an exile, he sailed to Cuba with the Revolutionary Directorate in February 1958 and joined its guerrilla front in the Escambray. Santiago became a commander in that column, which became part of the Rebel Army front led by Che Guevara in Las Villas. In October 1959, working for Cuban State Security, he pretended to break with the revolution in order to infiltrate the CIA-backed forces. He was killed by counterrevolutionary Cuban pirates in January 1961, as he was sailing toward Cuba to take up a CIA-appointed position as head of all armed counterrevolutionary forces in the Escambray.

Savimbi, Jonas (1934–) – In 1960, as a student, he joined an organization advocating the independence of Angola from Portuguese rule. In 1966 he founded the National Union for the Total Independence of Angola (UNITA). In 1975, as Portuguese colonial rule was collapsing, he allied himself with apartheid South Africa and U.S. imperialism in their efforts to overthrow the government of the newly independent country led by the Popular Movement for the Liberation of Angola (MPLA). Since then, UNITA has waged a terrorist war against the Angolan government, killing hundreds of thousands.

Second National Front of the Escambray – Armed group in Las Villas led by Eloy Gutiérrez Menoyo. The front was formed on November 10, 1957, on the initiative of the Revolutionary Directorate but betrayed the political goals of the Directorate and terrorized peasants in the Escambray, for which it was expelled from the Directorate in mid-1958. It refused to collaborate with Guevara's forces and other revolutionary units. Most of its leaders joined the counterrevolution after 1959.

Sékou Touré, Ahmed (1922–1984) – Leader of struggle for independence from France in what is today the Republic of Guinea. Became president of country at independence in 1958, serving until his death.

Soumialot, Gaston – A leader of the 1964–65 uprising in the Congo against the pro-imperialist regime. He was defense minister in the short-lived Congolese People's Republic proclaimed by the rebels in 1964.

Tartabul, Roberto (d. 1963) – Former member of the Rebel Army who was drummed out in early 1960s and later became a leader of a counterrevolutionary band in the Escambray. He was killed in battle in August 1963.

Tchamlesso, Godefroid (Tremendo Punto) – A leader of the Congolese anti-imperialist forces. Main Congolese leader in contact with the Cuban contingent led by Che Guevara. Currently living in Cuba.

Terry, Santiago (1930–1986) – Rebel Army combatant in the Sierra Maestra. He was one of the leaders of the Cuban contingent in the Congo in 1965 and was a colonel in the Revolutionary Armed Forces at the time of his death.

Tomassevich. See Menéndez Tomassevich, Raúl

Torres, Félix – Joined Communist Party in 1934. Led PSP guerrilla column in northern Las Villas, which put itself under the command of Camilo Cienfuegos. Became a commander in Rebel Army.

Trujillo, Rafael Leónidas (1891–1961) – Dictator in Dominican Republic from 1930 until his death. After 1959 he organized attacks against Cuba backed by Washington. He was assassinated by revolutionary opponents of the dictatorship.

Tshombe, Moise (1919–1969) – Led attempted breakaway of Katanga (now Shaba) province after the Congo won independence from Belgium in 1960. He helped organize the murder of Lumumba in 1961. Tshombe was prime minister of the Congo in 1964–65.

Union of Young Communists (UJC) – Born out of the Association of Rebel Youth (AJR) founded by the Rebel Army Department of Instruction in December 1959. Following a fusion of prorevolution youth organizations in October 1960, the AJR encompassed youth from the July 26 Movement, March 13 Revolutionary Directorate, and the Popular Socialist Party's Socialist Youth. It adopted the name UJC on April 4, 1962.

Valdés, Ramiro (1932–) – Participant in 1953 Moncada attack, he was sentenced to ten years in prison. Released May 1955 following amnesty campaign. A *Granma* expeditionary, he became second in command of Guevara's Rebel Army Column 4, later becoming its commander, and was second in command and later commander of Column 8 in Las Villas. He was minister of interior 1961–68, 1979–87. A member of Communist Party Central Committee since 1965, and of Political Bureau 1965–86.

Vargas, Luis (d. 1965) – One of the last bandits in the Escambray, he was captured, tried, and executed in December 1965.

Varona, Antonio (Tony) (1908–1992) – A leader of the Authentic Party, he served two terms as senator from Camagüey and was the prime minister of Cuba in 1948–50. After the revolution he left Cuba and was a figurehead in the Cuban Revolutionary Council, set up in 1961 at the initiative of the CIA to become a "provisional government" following the Bay of Pigs invasion.

Varona, Ricardo – A student who became a combatant in the Revolutionary Directorate guerrilla front in the Escambray. A captain in the Rebel Army, he participated in the attack on Placetas and other actions. He fought in the battle of Santa Clara. Prominent member of the Revolutionary Air Force after the victory of the revolution.

Villegas, Harry (Pombo) (1940–) – A native of Yara, in Oriente province, he joined the Rebel Army in 1957 and became a member of Che Guevara's personal escort in Columns 4 and 8. He served with Guevara in the Congo, where Che gave him the nom-de-guerre "Pombo," and later in Bolivia, where he was a member of the general staff of the guerrilla movement. After Guevara was killed in October 1967, Villegas commanded the group of surviving combatants that eluded the encirclement jointly organized by the Bolivian army and U.S. military forces, returning to Cuba in March 1968. He served three tours of duty in Angola in the 1970s and 1980s. He is currently a brigadier general in the Cuban armed forces no longer on active duty, a member of the Central Committee of the Communist Party, and heads the Patriotic, Military, and Internationalist Front of the Association of Combatants of the Cuban Revolution.

Walsh, Sinesio (d. 1960) – A member of the Rebel Army during the revolutionary war, he was promoted to captain after the revolution's victory and became squadron chief in Cruces. In August 1960 he helped organize a counterrevolutionary band in the Escambray and was captured, tried, and executed in October of that year.

Westbrook, Joe (1937–1957) – A youth leader of the Revolutionary Directorate and survivor of the March 13, 1957, attack on the Presidential Palace, he was murdered by Batista's police on April 20, in a massacre at 7 Humboldt St. in Havana.

Zayas, Alfonso (1936–) – Joined the Rebel Army in March 1957 and served as a captain in Column 8 under Guevara. After the victory of the revolution, he was political secretary of the Western Army, first secretary of the Communist Party in Las Tunas, and later an official in the Youth Army of Labor. Currently a brigadier general no longer on active duty and a leader of the Association of Combatants of the Cuban Revolution.

Zerquera, Rafael (Kumi) (1932–) – Served as a doctor in the internationalist contingent in the Congo in 1965, led by Che Guevara.

Index

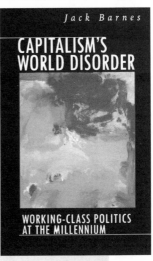

Capitalism's World Disorder

Working-class Politics at the Millennium
JACK BARNES

The social devastation and financial panic, the coarsening of politics, the cop brutality and acts of imperialist aggression accelerating around us—all are the product not of something gone wrong but of the lawful workings of capitalism. Yet the future can be changed by the united struggle and selfless action of workers and farmers conscious of their power to transform the world. $23.95

The Changing Face of U.S. Politics

Working-class Politics and the Trade Unions
JACK BARNES

Building the kind of party the working class needs to prepare for coming class battles—battles through which they will revolutionize themselves, their unions, and all of society. It is a companion volume to *Capitalism's World Disorder* for workers, farmers, and youth repelled by the class inequalities, economic instability, racism, women's oppression, cop violence, and wars endemic to capitalism, and who are determined to overturn that exploitative system and join in reconstructing the world on new, socialist foundations. $19.95

The Communist Manifesto

KARL MARX AND FREDERICK ENGELS

Founding document of the modern working-class movement, published in 1848. Explains why communism is derived not from preconceived principles but from *facts* and from proletarian movements springing from the actual class struggle. $3.95

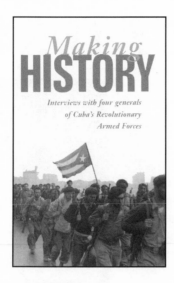

Making History

*Interviews with Four Generals of
Cuba's Revolutionary Armed Forces*

NÉSTOR LÓPEZ CUBA,
ENRIQUE CARRERAS,
JOSÉ RAMÓN FERNÁNDEZ,
HARRY VILLEGAS
Through the stories of four out-
standing Cuban generals, each
with close to half a century of
revolutionary activity, we can see
the class dynamics that have
shaped our entire epoch. We can
understand how the people of
Cuba, as they struggle to build a
new society, have for more than
forty years held Washington at
bay. $15.95

Episodes of the Cuban Revolutionary War, 1956–58

ERNESTO CHE GUEVARA
A firsthand account of the military campaigns
and political events that culminated in the
January 1959 popular insurrection that overthrew the U.S.-backed dictatorship in
Cuba. With clarity and humor, Guevara describes how the struggle transformed the
men and women of the Rebel Army and
July 26 Movement led by Fidel Castro. And
how these combatants forged a political
leadership capable of guiding millions of
workers and peasants to open the socialist
revolution in the Americas. $23.95

Playa Girón/Bay of Pigs

*Washington's First
Military Defeat in the Americas*

FIDEL CASTRO,
JOSÉ RAMÓN FERNÁNDEZ
In less than 72 hours of combat in April 1961, Cuba's revolutionary
armed forces defeated an invasion by 1,500 mercenaries organized
by Washington. In the process, the Cuban people set an example for
workers, farmers, and youth throughout the world that with political consciousness, class solidarity, unflinching courage, and revolutionary leadership, it is possible to stand up to enormous might and
seemingly insurmountable odds—and win. $20.00

Cuba and the Coming American Revolution

JACK BARNES

"There will be a victorious revolution in the United States before there will be a victorious counterrevolution in Cuba." That statement, made by Fidel Castro in 1961, remains as accurate today as when it was spoken. This book, which is about the class struggle in the imperialist heartland, explains why. $13.00

Cuba's Internationalist Foreign Policy

FIDEL CASTRO

Castro discusses the historic importance of the revolutionary victories won by the workers and farmers in Grenada and Nicaragua in 1979; Cuba's internationalist missions in Angola and Ethiopia; relations with Cubans living in the United States; and the proletarian internationalism that has guided the foreign policy of the Cuban government since 1959. $21.95

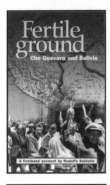

Fertile Ground

Che Guevara and Bolivia

A FIRSTHAND ACCOUNT
BY RODOLFO SALDAÑA

Told by one of the Bolivians who joined ranks with Guevara, Saldaña talks about the unresolved battles of the tin miners, peasants, and indigenous peoples of his country that created "fertile ground" for Guevara's revolutionary course and mark out the future of Bolivia and the Americas. $9.95

Che Guevara and the Imperialist Reality

MARY-ALICE WATERS

"The world of capitalist disorder—the imperialist reality of the 21st century—would not be strange to Che," Waters writes. "Far from being dismayed by the odds we face, he would have examined the world with scientific precision and charted a course to win." $3.50

The Cuban Revolution in the world

African freedom struggle

HOW FAR WE SLAVES HAVE COME!
South Africa and Cuba in Today's World
NELSON MANDELA, FIDEL CASTRO
> Speaking together in Cuba in 1991, Mandela and Castro discuss the unique relationship and example of the struggles of the South African and Cuban peoples. $9.95

THOMAS SANKARA SPEAKS
The Burkina Faso Revolution 1983–87
> Peasants and workers in the West African country of Burkina Faso established a popular revolutionary government and began to combat the hunger, illiteracy, and economic backwardness imposed by imperialist domination. Thomas Sankara, who led that struggle, explains the example set for all of Africa. $19.95

WOMEN'S LIBERATION
AND THE AFRICAN FREEDOM STRUGGLE
THOMAS SANKARA
> "There is no true social revolution without the liberation of women," explains the leader of the 1983–87 revolution in Burkina Faso. $5.00

AT THE SIDE OF CHE GUEVARA
INTERVIEWS WITH HARRY VILLEGAS (POMBO)

Currently a brigadier general in Cuba's Revolutionary Armed Forces, Villegas worked and fought alongside Ernesto Che Guevara for a decade—in Cuba, the Congo, and Bolivia. He talks about the struggles he has taken part in over four decades—including the 1988 defeat of the South African apartheid army at Cuito Cuanavale in Angola. $4.00

MALCOLM X TALKS TO YOUNG PEOPLE

"There is no better example of criminal activity against an oppressed people than the role the U.S. has been playing in the Congo," said Malcolm X in his January 1965 interview with the *Young Socialist* magazine, included in this collection. $10.95

REVOLUTION IN THE CONGO
DICK ROBERTS

Describes the 1960 victory of Congolese peasants and workers, led by Patrice Lumumba, against Belgian colonial rule. And the role, under United Nations cover, of Washington, Brussels, and other imperialist powers in the overthrow and assassination of Lumumba. $3.00

NELSON MANDELA SPEAKS
Forging a Democratic, Nonracial South Africa

Speeches from 1990–93 recounting the struggle that put an end to apartheid and opened the fight for a deepgoing political and social transformation in South Africa. $18.95

THE COMING REVOLUTION IN SOUTH AFRICA
JACK BARNES

Explores the social character and roots of apartheid in South African capitalism and the tasks of toilers in city and countryside in dismantling the legacy of class and racist inequality. Also includes "Why Cuban Volunteers Are in Angola," two speeches by Fidel Castro. In *New International* no. 5. $9.00

New International
A MAGAZINE OF MARXIST POLITICS AND THEORY

U.S. IMPERIALISM HAS LOST THE COLD WAR. That's what the Socialist Workers Party concluded at the opening of the 1990s, in the wake of the collapse of regimes and parties across Eastern Europe and in the USSR that claimed to be communist. Contrary to imperialism's hopes, the working class in those countries had not been crushed. It remains an intractable obstacle to reimposing and stabilizing capitalist relations, one that will have to be confronted by the exploiters in class battles—in a hot war.

Three issues of the Marxist magazine *New International* analyze the propertied rulers' failed expectations and chart a course for revolutionaries in response to rising worker and farmer resistance to the economic and social instability, spreading wars, and rightist currents bred by the world market system. They explain why the historic odds in favor of the working class have increased, not diminished, at the opening of the 21st century.

U.S. Imperialism
Has Lost the Cold War

JACK BARNES

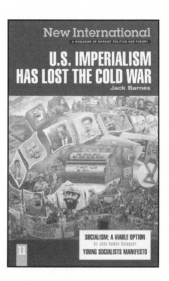

"It is only from fighters, from revolution-ists of action, that communists will be forged in the course of struggle. And it is only from within the working class that the mass political vanguard of these fight-ers can come. The lesson from over 150 years of political struggle by the modern workers movement is that, more and more, to become and remain a revolu-tionist means becoming a communist." In *New International* no. 11. **$14.00**

Imperialism's March toward Fascism and War

JACK BARNES

"There will be new Hitlers, new Mussolinis. That is inevitable. What is not inevitable is that they will triumph. The working-class vanguard will orga-nize our class to fight back against the devastating toll we are made to pay for the capitalist crisis. The future of humanity will be decided in the contest between these contending class forces." In *New International* no. 10. **$14.00**

Opening Guns of World War III

JACK BARNES

"Washington's Gulf war and its outcome did not open up a new world order of stability and UN-overseen harmony. Instead, it was the first war since the close of World War II that grew primarily out of the intensified competition and accelerating instability of the crises-ridden old imperial-ist world order." In *New International* no. 7. **$12.00**

ALSO AVAILABLE IN *New International's* SISTER PUBLICATIONS
IN SPANISH, FRENCH, AND SWEDISH

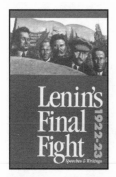

Lenin's Final Fight
Speeches and Writings, 1922–23
V.I. LENIN
In the early 1920s Lenin waged a political battle in the leadership of the Soviet Union to maintain the course that had enabled workers and peasants to overthrow the tsarist empire, carry out the first socialist revolution, and launch a world communist movement. The issues posed in this fight—from the party's class composition, to the worker-peasant alliance and battle against national oppression—remain central to world politics today. $19.95

By Any Means Necessary
MALCOLM X
"Why should we do the dirtiest jobs for the lowest pay? I'm telling you we do it because we have a rotten system. It's a political and economic system of exploitation, of outright humiliation, degradation, discrimination."
—Malcolm X, June 1964. $15.95

Cointelpro
The FBI's Secret War on Political Freedom
NELSON BLACKSTOCK
The decades-long covert spying and disruption program directed at socialists and activists in the Black and anti-Vietnam War movements. Includes FBI documents. $15.95

The Working Class and the Transformation of Learning
The Fraud of Education Reform under Capitalism
JACK BARNES
"Until society is reorganized so that education is a human activity from the time we are very young until the time we die, there will be no education worthy of working, creating humanity." $3.00